LETTERS TO MY BROTHERS AND SISTERS

Donald J. Goergen, OP

Dominican Publications

Table of Contents

This edition first published (1996) by
Dominican Publications, 42 Parnell Square,
Dublin 1, Ireland.

ISBN 1-871552-57-5

British Library Cataloguing in Publication Data.
A catalogue record for this book is available from
the British Library

THE ILLUSTRATIONS

On the cover, a reproduction of a stained glass window in the chapel of St
Dominic's house, Fanjeaux, France, by Jean Hugo. Legend says that on
three successive nights in July 1206, from Fanjeaux, a hill-town, St
Dominic saw the *Seignadou*, a globe of flame come to rest over a ruined
church in nearby Prouille. He then knew that his mission was to begin in
southern France and that Prouille and its nuns were to be central to it.

By Albert Carpentier, OP: pages 11, 23, 53, 73, 79, 107, 136. Fr
Carpentier, member of the Canadian Province, lives in Tokyo, Japan.

By Mary Ansgar, OP: pages 17, 20, 41, 43, 47. Sr Mary Ansgar, of the
Congregation of St Catherine of Siena (Stone), England, died last year in
one of the Congregation's convents in Norway.

By Placid Stuckenschneider, OSB: pages 33, 57, 64, 84. Br Placid is a
member of St John's Abbey, Collegeville, Minnesota. The drawings were
published in *The Dominicans*, Liturgical Press, and are reproduced by
kind permission.

By Henri Matisse, page 54. M. Matisse created the chapel of the Rosary,
Vence, between 1949 and 1951. He died in 1954.

By Mary Grace, OP, page 113. Sr Mary Grace is a member of St
Dominic's Monastery, Washington, DC.

Cover design by David Cooke, Dublin.

Origination by Dominican Publications

Printed by Versa Press, Inc., East Peoria, Illinois.

Foreword

To write a letter, even to a group one knows well, is a risk. One is conscious that one's truth is partial, that what is said arises from particular concerns and experiences, that words "slip, slide, perish, decay with imprecision" (T.S Eliot, *Burnt Norton*). Unlike a conversation, there is no immediate feedback, no ready opportunity to hear and consider disagreement, to identify and clarify misunderstandings, to reach deeper mutual understanding. Words disembodied of voice and gesture reach the readers silently. Writing is particularly challenging when one has a sense of the whole group, the spectrum of ideologies, contexts, temperaments, concerns, histories. In a single act, one reaches out to the afflicted and the comfortable, sensates and intuitives, innovators and traditionalists.

Yet letters are a vital way in which religious leaders fulfill their unique function of reflecting back to the group a sense of the whole. They are a way of serving the community by naming critical issues, offering a context for their consideration, and raising questions for personal reflection and communal dialogue. Because letters can be read and re-read, they may be friendly companions on the adventure which Donald Goergen, OP, calls "continuous formation." If they are done well, they are a means whereby a religious leader can perform what Herbert McCabe, OP, terms the job of the superior: "to play the central role in an educational process by which the good for the house becomes clear to everyone" (*New Blackfriars*, June, 1984).

The effectiveness of these letters is determined by the degree to which they foster conversion in the writer and readers, elicit dangerous memories, awaken recognition, unsettle routines, soothe the heart, strengthen the lonely, seed questions, provoke debate, move to prayer, evoke a chuckle. Such letters have served their function if they have promoted the vitality of the tradition which gives the community its distinctive identity and purpose, opened a common ground, helped to achieve a common sense and effectively oriented the community to the common good. In Catholic theological tradition, this process is known as reception. It is the recognition of the truth in a way that forms a community of greater freedom and solidarity. The decision of the Dominican Friars of St. Albert the Great Province, to whom these letters were addressed, to have them published is one measure of their reception.

To make these letters available to a group beyond their original audience is no less a risk. What word of insight and liberation might they speak to other readers? Are they so bound to their context that they have only a limited appeal?

This volume will find a natural audience in other Dominicans, both women and men, because its letters and addresses are a sustained reflection on elements of the Dominican charism: preaching, common life, contemplation, study. In exploring these topics, Goergen makes fresh connections between contemporary issues and Dominican tradition. His 1987 address to the Provincial Assembly, "Preaching in Solidarity with the God of Jesus Christ" is a particularly moving example of his ability to bring insights from the Order's intellectual tradition to bear on the relationship between holiness and justice. In doing so, he furthers that tradition.

Beyond the Dominican Family, this volume may be useful to women and men religious in a variety of contexts. Goergen's reflections on the vows and the common life, on the option for the poor and on conversion are food for personal thought and springboards for communal dialogue. His final letter, "Religious Life and the Gospel," is a stimulating and highly original contribution to the theology of religious life.

With compassion, honesty and delicate balance, Goergen takes on some of the critical, even divisive, issues in contemporary religious life in the United States: preaching justice; community and intimacy; activism and contemplation; the lure of individualism and materialism; pluralism and diversity within a faith community; how to identify ministerial priorities without succumbing to uniformity. Had these letters been written by the head of a community of women, the contents would probably have included a treatment of the issues raised by feminism, rather than the challenge to clericalism found in Goergen's letter on the laity.

This volume is, at its heart, an example of fine preaching. Its contents flow from reflection on Scripture and tradition, engagement in contemporary issues and deep love for the church and for a particular community. They demonstrate a knowledge of history and current magisterial teaching. It is preaching which has passed through the crucible of experience and contemplation and which invites a response of dialogue and conversion. Such preaching has power to move many other women and men hungering for insight and thirsting for holiness.

Patricia Walter, OP
Prioress, Adrian Dominican Sisters
June 20, 1995

Preface

The letters in this volume were originally written to my Dominican brothers in the Province of St. Albert the Great, USA. Our Provincial Chapter of 1994, judging them to have value beyond the province and also beyond the Dominican Family, asked that they be published in order to make them more widely available. I am deeply appreciative. We have entitled this collection, *Letters to My Brothers and Sisters*, yet one must always keep in mind the original context as that of a provincial writing his brothers. I was provincial from 1985-1994. The letters (and two addresses) included here cover a range of issues pertinent to the future of religious life.

The years of leadership were not easy. I have no regrets about having accepted the responsibility. They were both demanding and rewarding years. During them I came to formulate my own definition of leadership as a process of being drawn more deeply into the mystery of discipleship. Leadership is living the paschal mystery. It is a privilege. It is a cross. I am glad I picked it up. I was glad to lay it down.

I love my brothers and sisters in the Dominican family. I am proud of them. I came to know how fragile we really are.

Every person's spiritual journey is distinctive — the path by which we are drawn into being servants of humanity and servants of God. Mine may have gotten a jump starts from an asthmatic attack as a child. My parents were Iowa farmers. I had asthma, so I wasn't destined to be a farmer. But I liked school. I wanted to spend the rest of my life in school. It was a Catholic school. Franciscan sisters taught me. So already at an early age I hoped that God was calling me to priesthood. Thus I could stay in school by being a teacher. Intimations of a call trying to break through!

I didn't always make it easy for God, nor did God always make it easy for me. I tried the diocesan priesthood, but my vocation was to Dominican life. I remain grateful to the Province for receiving me. The two and a half years between my departure from the diocesan seminary and entering the Order were important and maturing years. They took me to Kentucky, back to Iowa, then Berkeley, California and Topeka, Kansas before I became a novice with the friars preachers.

Religious life at this period of history is not easy. A few years ago I summarized mine as: God, 4; Goergen, 0. Almost always what I had chosen for a ministry was not what God had chosen for me. In retrospect, however, God had the better plan.

A difficult thing about being provincial is that one has to care for a personal life as well as a public one. It is not always easy to be attentive to the former. In 1992 my Mom died. In 1994 Dad died shortly after my second term was over. I now miss them — especially now that I might have had more time to spend with them.

Another difficult thing about being provincial is the misconception that you set the agenda. People think of leadership as power. There is a power in it, but not the one we ordinarily think of. My own goals and plans frequently had to be altered. What I wanted to do or was elected to do or simply had to do were seldom the same. Leadership itself requires a profound obediential listening.

It is still too soon for me to say what I have learned. I know that I was changed by this ministry as by my previous ones. One feels called to be obedient to truth. It is difficult to speak the truth, to do the truth, to seek truth with love. It was truth that changed me and set me free. I felt compelled to live for the sake of the gospel, and not just an ideology. I often felt put to the test. Was my deepest commitment to the agenda of the left, or the agenda of the right? In the struggles one has to learn that there is a reality beyond both. I call that gospel. My understanding of the gospel, and of religious life in relationship to the gospel, was there in the beginning, but one can also see that it developed over these nine years.

At some point I hope to articulate more clearly what I have learned. At this point I am simply grateful to you, my brothers and sisters with whom I share gospel life, and to whom I dedicate these reflections. I especially thank Marygrace Peters, OP, for her assistance in editing, Lucy Sanchez for her typing, and Patricia Walter, OP, for her willingness to write a foreword.

Donald J. Goergen, OP
June 24, 1995, Feast of the Birth of St. John the Baptist

1, Preaching[1]

Dear Brothers,

The feast of our founder and brother Dominic is here. This occasion calls for celebration, but the summer date does not always find us at home. Wherever you are, may the strength and peace and joy of Dominic be with each of you.

The feast of Dominic calls for more than celebration. It is also an occasion for reflecting on our mission. We honor our founder by focusing on the gift Dominic gave to the Church: preaching. To follow Dominic means to be for our period of history what Dominic was for his. The Dominican family is missionary; our lives are apostolic. This is always the starting point for our self-understanding and for renewing our lives.

Dominic was always a lover of God, of Jesus Christ, and of the Church. And he became in time a lover of preaching. From Caleruega in Old Castile to the University of Bologna, from the episcopal town of Osma to the papal see in Rome, through the towns of the diocese of Toulouse, Dominic gradually found his voice as a preacher. He was convinced of the power and importance of preaching for the Church, and his love of preaching prompted him to gather together a community of preachers, his gift to the Church.

Dominic's life was shaped as much by the Pope's agenda and by the yearnings of his times as by his own. Innocent III had called for preachers. He had looked first to Cistercian monks, but something new was demanded at that moment in history. It had not yet been conceived, but it came about through Dominic Guzman and his companions. New wine could not be contained in old wineskins. Between his encounter with the Cistercian preachers at Montpellier in the summer of 1206 and his death in the summer of 1221, Dominic gave birth — gradual, uncertain, but deliberate — to the Preachers. From 1206 on, Dominic himself was formed by that project. After Bishop Diego died at the end of 1207, the urgent preaching mission fell to Dominic. He was not yet forty years old. It was only then, after so many years in the shadow of Diego, that his own vocation flowered with the formation of a new missionary, preaching, religious family in the Church.

The early sources of our history show how earnestly Dominic desired the confirmation of an order which would be called an Order of Preachers (see Jordan of Saxony, *Beginnings of the Order of Preachers*, 40). In

---

1. August 8, 1985, Feast of St. Dominic

asking for such a title, Dominic was asking for a lot. There already was an *ordo praedicatorum* in the Church. It was the episcopal order! Yet Dominic sought both the name and the mission: he wanted his religious family to be and to be known as Preachers. His goal was realized and officially confirmed, the order on December 22, 1216, and the name shortly thereafter (see Vicaire, *St. Dominic and His Times*, pp. 217-25).

In fidelity to our founder and our tradition, our own identity and spirituality must derive from the preaching mission. It is our charism and our gift. It is arguable that decline and renewal in the Dominican Family mirror quite accurately the weakening and strengthening of our responsiveness to that *gratia praedicationis*. The question returns: what does it mean for us to be preachers, not at the beginning of the thirteenth century, but at the end of the twentieth?

Granted the diversity of our personalities and particular works, preaching remains the gift that unites us in a brotherhood and a family. It gives a distinctive character or shape to our differing ministries and calls them (and us) into cooperation within the Church. What does it mean to be a Preacher who is a teacher or a theologian, or a pastoral minister in a parish or hospital or on a campus, someone working for peace and justice, an administrator, or a full-time itinerant preacher? We are all Preachers, but not everything we do is preaching, yet preaching ought to help form everything we do.

Asking and attempting to answer the question of what being a Preacher means today activates the spiritual and theological life of the preacher. It reaches into our deepest motives and touches upon our faith. Preaching makes a theological life necessary. Thomas Aquinas wrote the *Summa Contra Gentiles* as a collaborative preaching, we might say, with and for his brother Dominicans. Theology gives content to our preaching, and preaching gives shape to our theology.

Any theology of preaching must clearly be a theology of the Word, intimately related to theologies of the Trinity, Christ, the Spirit and the Church. For various reasons, not all of them unfortunate, our theological understandings of these central mysteries differ in varying ways, but they come together in our common desire to proclaim the Word and in the traditions that comprise our Catholicism. Our varying theologies give Dominican preaching many facets, many voices. They make our common mission intelligible in a society that is of many different, conflicting minds.

As the Dominican Family, given the charism of preaching, we must be a community that is characterized by prayer, thought and articulate expression. A deepening theological and spiritual life brings together the

Dominic "was convinced of the power and importance of preaching for the Church." (p. 9)

Artist, ALBERT CARPENTIER, OP

reality of God and the lives of God's people. Profound fidelity to this vocation is far more important to our own unity in the Order than any conformity in theological stances or forms of ministry. And it is absolutely essential to the effectiveness of our ministries in the Church.

Our reflection on our vocation should include self-examination. What are we doing and how well are we doing it?

How is my particular ministry related to our corporate mission? How do I preach the gospel? Is the gospel central to my prayer, thought, and life?

How do I try to improve my own effectiveness as a preacher? Assuming that my preaching can always be better than it is, how have I taken responsibility for my continuing formation as a preacher? Where does my preaching need improvement?

Is my preaching substantively, doctrinally weak? Could it (I) benefit from more study? Am I saying the same things today that I did five years ago? Repeating ideas that have not deepened or developed?

Or, is my preaching substantive and doctrinal, but spiritually lifeless? Does the power of the Holy Spirit manifest itself in my words? Is my preaching grounded in prayer? Am I preaching my own ideas (myself), or Jesus Christ?

Or, do I rely solely on the power of the Holy Spirit without enough attention to some basic human skills? Have I shifted all the responsibility to God and neglected what I might learn from others' feedback, or from a preaching workshop?

Do I evaluate what I do? Allow others to give me straight feedback? Is my preaching grounded in humility, poverty of spirit and accurate self-knowledge?

What are the human experiences which form me and my words? Have I any experience of material poverty, dependence, solidarity with the poor of this world? How have I allowed the cry of the poor, those without social status, education or power, to influence my understanding of the gospel and my expression of it?

For Dominic, preaching was founded in a life of poverty, prayer and study. Is that true of me and my preaching?

Considering our corporate mission of preaching, I see three particular tasks confronting us in the next few years:

1. Our continuing formation as preachers: the ways in which we accept responsibility for personal and corporate development as effective, grace-filled preachers.

2. The development of our communities as centers of preaching. How can our particular manner of living together directly promote the prayer, study and expression that comprise our preaching and publicly identify us as "Preachers"?

3. Collaboration with our Dominican sisters in the preaching mission and the promotion of lay preaching in the Church. That our sisters have recognized and accepted their share in the charism of Dominic is an impressive fact of our times.

Given the centrality of preaching in the mission of the earthly Jesus (Mark 1:38), given its centrality in the life and mission of Dominic, and given the needs of our world and Church today, let us approach the feast of Dominic as a time for celebration, reflection, and self-evaluation. Let us approach the feast with our lives focused on our mission. Let us celebrate the feast as Preachers.

Fraternally in our brother Dominic,
Don

2, Faith, Politics and Justice[1]

Dear Brothers,

Every saint discloses some aspect of the mystery of grace, and every Dominican saint some aspect of the mystery of Dominican life, lived in its fullness only by all of us together. We are approaching the feast of Friar Albert of Cologne, our Dominican brother and Province patron. Albert's life reflects several facets of the Dominican spirit. We have Albert the teacher, the *doctor universalis*, the patron of scientists, and the exponent of Aristotelianism. Albert was indeed a man of learning, intellectual inquisitiveness, a life-long student. But the Albert I ponder today is the Albert captured in the nickname by which many Bavarians knew him: Bishop Boots.

During his three years as provincial, Albert made formal visitations of all the houses in the province on foot (as was the custom for the friars preachers). "It was Albert's custom while travelling — always by foot — first to visit the chapel of the religious house where he intended to stay the night, to thank God for the safe journey, then immediately to visit the library to see whether there were any books there that he had not yet seen" (James A. Weisheipl, "The Life and Works of St. Albert the Great," in *Albertus Magnus and the Sciences, Commemorative Essays 1980,* ed. James A. Weisheipl, Toronto, 1980, p. 34).

Albert never desired to be provincial, nor bishop. He was allowed to resign from both. As bishop he continued to live the life of Dominican simplicity: his preferential option for Dominican poverty. Although permitted as bishop to ride horseback, Bishop Boots visited the whole of his diocese on foot. Albert was a man of both learning and poverty. The one did not exclude the other. Thus, as we celebrate the feast of Albert, I would like to reflect on our call to preach justice — a call rooted in both learning and true poverty.

FAITH AND POLITICS

In my previous letter, I spoke about our preaching mission. Preaching, theological education, and justice have been clearly set as Province priorities for some years now (See Acts of the Provincial Chapter, 1977, n. 85). Neither the ministry of preaching nor the challenge of theological education can be severed from one of the clearest signs of our time: the cry of the poor.

1. November 15, 1985, Feast of St. Albert the Great

Justice is not only a human, social concern. It is a concern of faith as well. Indeed, it is a moral imperative, not an option. Justice talk disturbs us because it has political implications, and many of us prefer to think of ourselves as non-political, at least in so far as we speak as representatives of the Church. Justice talk also raises economic questions, about which we must humbly acknowledge a lack of expertise. Yet we cannot escape the thirst for justice in our world without rendering the gospel and the teachings of the Church vacuous.

Rather, we must assert strongly to one another and to the people whom we serve the inseparable connections among faith, justice, politics, and economics.

As United States citizens, we have grown up with the idea of the separation of church and state, and we see the wisdom in such a separation, and we rightly attempt to protect it. Yet, at the same time that we say "Separation of the church and state, yes," we must also say, "Separation of faith and politics, no." Separating the practice of the faith from the socio-political issues which confront our world is not only undesirable but impossible. One cannot desire to be non-political as a man or woman of faith unless one desires the faith to be socially irrelevant.

Justice thus remains a constituent element of our preaching. And we must educate people who accept the separation of church and state about the inseparability of faith and political life. We must insist that faith does not pre-determine or dictate concrete, prudential, political and economic decisions. The gospel does not tell us what we must do in all the concrete circumstances of life. But the gospel does teach us that political and economic issues are moral issues as well. Politics and economics are not value-free, devoid of moral concerns. The strong reaction among some against the United States Bishops' pastoral letter on peace and the upcoming pastoral on the United States economy,[2] arguing that bishops have no expertise or right to speak on political and economic topics, indicates that United States Catholics have been improperly taught or at least unconsciously allowed to assume that political and economic decisions can be non-moral. Perhaps this will be one of the major contributions of the bishops' recent pastorals: making us aware that social, political, and economic decisions are moral decisions as well.

Faith seeks after justice; the social, political, and economic responsibility of the Christian cannot be denied. This responsibility is not the whole of the gospel, but it is essential to the gospel. We too often err by

2. This was published in 1986, its title *Economic Justice for All.*

going in one of two directions, by reducing the gospel to social justice alone, or by denying the intrinsic link between the gospel and justice. There is no gospel without the challenge to act justly, and yet there is more to the gospel than justice by itself alone.

In its wisdom, the Church advocates no particular economic system. As church we realize our compatibility with a variety of economic systems and the historical expressions thereof. Systems are criticized when they violate basic human rights. Such violations the Church as God's people cannot tolerate — not because it is making concrete prudential moral decisions for its members but because the Church sees itself as an advocate for human dignity. This value runs through the bishops' pastoral, the writings of John Paul II, the modern social teaching of the Church, back to medieval and patristic times. The Church sees itself as an advocate for the common good.

The Church in France in the nineteenth century had to come to grips with modern political systems and political democracy. The Church had to come to the awareness that to be a Catholic did not necessitate being a monarchist. The Church struggled with these issues, now considered dated, and in so doing lost many of the people, much of the working class. Our own Henri Lacordaire contributed to the acceptance of the democratic form of government. So, in the twentieth century, the Church faces the challenge of coming to grips with new economic systems as well. Where are our Lacordaires?

A PROVINCE SEEKING JUSTICE

We affirm the separation of church and state as well as the inseparability of faith and politics. Economic issues are moral issues, yet we respect the prudential area and peoples' moral decision-making. We speak out against the violations of human rights. We seek to learn what it means to be compatible with non-capitalist economic systems. All this is fraught with danger, but the virtue of justice cannot be separated from the virtues of "courage" and "good sense." (See Herbert McCabe, *The Teaching of the Catholic Church.*)

Perhaps our failures with respect to justice pertain as readily to these other two moral virtues. How many of us seek justice deeply in our hearts, but lack the courage it takes to speak out, preach, or act on behalf of justice? We are people of good will, but also cowards. Or our particular failure may be a lack of good sense. How often do we not see the words or deeds of others as providing no role models because they are rooted in self-righteousness, single issues, or a simple lack of wisdom? As Preachers we seek justice, but a justice undergirded by courage and good sense.

Certainly as preachers, as educators, as people who have committed ourselves to the practice and the preaching of Christian life in its fullness, we are at a point in our own history where we can and must take the pursuit of justice even more seriously. I grant that we will all have our own opinions on political and economic questions. I also grant that recognizing the social implications of the gospel opens the door to politicizing our life together; it can be a source of tension and disunity.

I do not grant, however, that differences of opinion are bad for us, that differences need necessarily negate the deeper bonds of brotherhood that we share, that adult religious are incapable of genuine human respect for those who disagree with them. We do not need to avoid discussions about the socio-political implications of the gospel. What we need to avoid are: (1) an arrogant attitude that one is always right, and (2) quick, unreflective solutions to extremely complex issues. We do not need to disagree with one another less; we need to understand one another more. We need to avoid the ready-at-hand ways of categorizing people and defining ourselves over against each other, intellectuals over against activists, contemplatives over against prophets, men over against women, liberals over against conservatives, and we could go on. We all have something to contribute and we all must contribute to the search for a more just society.

A Dominican pursuit of justice is inseparable from our pursuit of truth, our obligation to study, our capacity to reflect in common. We cannot justify being ignorant in the areas of greatest concern to our contemporary world. We must do the truth as we seek the truth. Justice and truth are never opposed.

"Albert the teacher, the doctor universalis, patron of scientists." (p. 14).

Artist, MARY ANSGAR, OP

When we speak of peace and justice as a ministry, we do so in at least three ways, and all three are valid and necessary. In the first, most restricted sense, we think of our brothers who have committed them-selves on a full-time basis to direct action on behalf of peace and economic justice. In a second sense, we think of those who have given themselves full-time to more traditional, institutional apostolates, but apostolates that are clearly on behalf of the poor. Among others, I think of the majority of our parishes. In a third, even less restricted, but equally important sense, we think of all of us for whom peace and justice must be an essential part of our apostolic life: at the level of provincial leadership, in parish ministry or at campus centers, in our preaching, teaching, scholarship, music, art, counselling, and administration. These, too, must be ministries for justice.

We are not all involved in the peace and justice ministry in the same way, but we must all be committed to peace and justice as a constitutive element in our ministries. How does the cry of the poor inform our preaching? Being able to preach justice and peace is both difficult and necessary, avoiding the two extremes of platitudes and partisanship. The same is true of us as educators. The concern for justice must be a part of our teaching, research, or administrative activities. Does the parish have its peace and justice committee and is it given a central role in pastoral planning? Have we all read the first drafts of the bishops' pastoral on the United States economy so that we can implement the final draft in our communities and ministries? In the worship life of a community, bap-tism, reconciliation, and Eucharist are all occasions for raising our social consciousness and deepening our faith.

These three senses in which we are committed to peace and justice pertain primarily to our individual ministries. But there are also ways in which we are called to act corporately. The Provincial Chapter recom-mended that the Province take corporate stances on important issues related to peace and justice (1985 Acts of the Provincial Chapter, n.30) in accord with approved guidelines. This makes us aware of corporate as well as individual social responsibilities.

THE BISHOPS' PASTORAL

Individually and corporately, it is not a question of whether but of how to involve ourselves in the political, economic, and social issues of our day, not because we are more knowledgeable than laity but because we share responsibility with the laity for our world, God's world. The practice of the faith cannot be limited to nor separated from societal issues.

As Dominican preachers, educators, and pastors we must be prepared to promote the pastoral, "Catholic Social Teaching and the US Economy." The final draft is scheduled to be approved in the Fall of 1986. The second draft is already a shorter, more concise statement. If we do not read it carefully and follow its development, we will not be prepared when the final draft is approved.[3]

In the first drafts, several points in particular are worth highlighting.

1. The bishops have made an option for solidarity with the poor and are challenging us to follow their lead. Concern for the needs of the poor and the vulnerable is to be a primary guiding economic principle.

2. The approach taken in the pastoral reflects the more recent pastoral and theological methodology developing in the Church which begins with a reading of "the signs of the times," social analysis, dialogue and consultation "from below".

3. One of the major contributions of the pastoral will be to alert us to the reality that economic issues and decisions are moral issues and decisions as well. "Therefore we want to call all persons, no matter what their income or status, to a new commitment to economic justice. Such a commitment is an inescapable implication of belief in Jesus Christ".

4. The pastoral does not deal explicitly with the capitalism vs. socialism debate. Yet it recognizes that contemporary forms of capitalism can make a virtue out of fallen human nature and take advantage of our sinful selves by structurally building upon them: consumerism.

5. The Church recognizes that it has, as an institution, moral obligations in the economic sphere. "All the moral principles that govern the just operation of any economic endeavor apply to the church and its many agencies and institutions; indeed the church should be exemplary."

6. Lying underneath the pastoral is a new definition or understanding of holiness. It is this that may be the most difficult for traditionally educated Christians to grasp or accept, but what may be most important for us to see, namely, that holiness involves a commitment to justice, even if it cannot be reduced to that alone.

These points, solidarity with the poor, a consultative methodology, the moral dimension of economic life, the limitations of capitalism, principles of justice as applicable to the church, and a new understanding of holiness must help to shape our consciousness and our preaching.

3. See note 2.

We celebrate the feast of Albert the Great with great respect for our Dominican intellectual heritage as well as for our Dominican contribution to Catholic social thought and social action. We especially call to mind Bishop Boots' love of poverty as we are called in our own period of history to make that option for solidarity with the poor. May the feast of Albert be an occasion for celebration, self-reflection, and just preaching. May it bring us closer into solidarity with the poor.

Fraternally in Dominic and Albert,
Don

"our own family album of memories captured in word and fresco, in wood, stone and bronze." (p. 127).
Head of Dominic by Mary Ansgar, OP, after the thirteenth century wooden sculpture in Prouille, France.

3, Mission, Ministry, and Continuing Formation[1]

Dear Brothers,

Thomas Aquinas has continuing value not only for the synthesis he once effected but also as a model thinker. Thomas must be understood as a truly *biblical* theologian. This does not mean that he was not also a speculative theologian. But we can easily forget his career of lecturing on the Scriptures and his commentaries on Job, the Psalms, the Song of Songs, Isaiah, Jeremiah, Matthew, John, and the letters of Paul. Thomas was a master of the Scriptures. In his *Summa*, he sides with opinions that the Scriptures seem to more readily endorse. The major question for Thomas as a theologian was simply what opinion is most in accord with the Scriptures.

Thomas must also be understood as a *continually developing* and open theologian. Thomas never stopped thinking! His theology is not simply a finished product but also a creative inquiry still going on toward the end of his life when he decided to discontinue writing. On the question of whether God would have become incarnate if humankind had not sinned, Thomas grew in his understanding and changed his mind between his writing of the *Sentences* (1252-1256) and the later *tertia pars* of the *Summa* (begun around Spring of 1272). On the significant question in Thomas' Christology of whether there was only one *esse* in Christ, or whether Christ as a human being has an *esse* as well, Thomas shows himself as continually thinking. He changes his mind within one year, age forty-seven or forty-eight, between the disputation *De unione verbi incarnati* written earlier in 1272 and the famous question 17 of the *tertia pars* later in that year. There are many such examples. Thomas was capable of continual thinking and rethinking and changing his mind.

Thomas' theology, while scholastic, was also *pastoral* — intended to be a guide for the preachers of the Order. The history of the preaching friars, as far back as Dominic, was wrapped up with the struggle against the Albigensians. Thomas sought out and then thought out a theology that might more effectively aid "The Preaching." He chose Aristotle to assist him in developing a theology of creation and nature in response to Manicheism.

Thomas sets the example for us, along with other values, of what it means to be *a biblical, pastoral, and continually developing thinker*.

1. January 28, 1986, Feast of St. Thomas Aquinas

OUR MISSION AND MINISTRY

Among the concerns that our Province frequently raises are those of ministerial planning and provincial identity. Who are we, and what are we about? A fairly straightforward answer can be given to the question. We are preachers, educators, and promoters of peace and justice. This does not mean a lessened commitment to campus, parochial, or other provincial commitments. It does mean that ministry in these settings ought to emphasize quality preaching, educational programming, and the promotion of justice and peace.

Our conscientious commitment to preaching, education, and justice reflect not only a long Dominican heritage but also our more recent provincial decisions. The acts of our 1977 Chapter stated:

> We recommend that there be no priority ranking of individual ministries, but that three areas of ministry are especially suited to the Dominican mission. These areas might function as guidelines for the brethren, the provincial and the Council, and for Formation personnel. They are:
> 1. the preaching ministries in their variety of forms;
> 2. the intellectual and artistic ministries;
> 3. the social ministries in which the Gospel is brought to the less advantaged and oppressed. (1977 ACTS, n. 85)

We confuse ourselves if we talk about provincial "priorities" in terms of numbers — as if we can really determine how many brothers are committed to quality preaching, learning, and social change by counting numbers. The Province really has two priorities: ministry and continuing formation. These are two interdependent efforts. Like inhaling and exhaling, one is not more important than the other.

Preaching, theological education, and the promotion of justice are not the priorities of the Province as much as they are the means by which we understand, articulate, and implement our mission. They are what I prefer to call apostolic *norms*. "Norms" refer not so much to common practice, as to those actions or aspirations in terms of which we choose to understand who we are and what we are about.

Aidan Kavanagh explains:
> A *norm* in this sense has nothing to do with the number of times a thing is done, but it has everything to do with the standard according to which a thing is done. So long as the norm is in place both in practice and in the awareness of those who are engaged in it, the situation is capable of being judged "normal" even though the norm must be

"Thomas sought out and then thought out a theology that might more effectively aid 'The Preaching'." (p. 21)

Artist, Albert Carpentier, OP

departed from to some extent, even frequently, due to exigencies of time, place, pastoral considerations, physical inabilities, or whatever. Yet to the extent possible, the norm must always be achieved to some extent lest it slip imperceptibly into the status of a mere ideal all wish for but are under no obligation to realize. (Aidan Kavanagh, The Shape of Baptism, Pueblo, 108.)

Ministry is one of the two priorities of the province. And there are three primary apostolic norms in terms of which we understand our ministry: preaching, education, and justice. These three do not confine the apostolic life or ministries in the Province but rather define how we understand and interpret ourselves.

Ministry articulated in terms of these norms is clearly to be encouraged; ministries less clearly related to this apostolic self-understanding are less encouraged. But these are norms in terms of which all of us can and ought to evaluate our apostolic lives. A particular teacher who is unconcerned about the quality of his preaching, who sees little connection between teaching and the proclamation of the Word, whose style or message do not contribute to more just social relationships does not honor the Dominican vocation simply by teaching. A pastor or chaplain is a better Dominican to the extent that he exercises his ministry in effective preaching, and takes every opportunity for evangelization, adult catechesis, and the active pursuit of peace and justice.

CONTINUING FORMATION

In contrast to the priority of ministry which I have spoken about in terms of three apostolic norms, I prefer to speak about continuing formation in terms of questions which we must continue to discuss.

What does it mean for us to be brothers to each other?

How do we relate our brotherhood to the wider context of the Dominican family and collaboration with our Dominican sisters?

How are questions of brotherhood, collaboration, and priesthood rooted in the ongoing challenge of conversion, deepening, and renewal in our common life?

Brotherhood, collaboration, priesthood, and renewal are all rooted in continuing formation.

Renewal cannot be discussed in the abstract, but must be related to the concrete, existential areas of our common life: prayer, study, obedience, poverty, chastity. These are all areas for continuing renewal that we must take up one by one, re-examine, and re-own. Our apostolic life is rooted in our common life; the renewal of one requires the renewal of the other.

Ultimately, both the priority of ministry and the priority of continuing formation are rooted in one goal: charity, as St. Thomas so clearly affirms, a growth in charity that manifests itself in friendship, brotherhood, collaboration, and ministry.

OUR INTELLECTUAL TRADITION

As Dominicans, we take pride in our intellectual history. Our history, however, carries with it a responsibility. What we have received we hand on to the future as a living tradition. There are two tendencies that we must always check lest they distort our tradition rather than enhance it: the tendency toward elitism and the tendency toward rationalism. The correctives lie in seeing that our intellectual tradition is both pastoral and contemplative.

Dominican reflection is related to the realities of this world. Its concerns are human, social, and pastoral. Dominic addressed his preaching to the needs of his world and church, his period of history. The crisis of Albigensianism was not an abstract theological problem but a pressing social and pastoral issue. The same was true for Thomas. His *Summa Contra Gentiles* was to serve as an aid to his preaching brothers challenged by an increased awareness of the world of Islam. And we can say the same for Catherine: a woman for all times because she was first of all a woman of her times. Our intellectual heritage is not an intellectualism that separates us from others and makes us aloof, but rather an appreciation of critical thought that flows out of our deep pastoral sensitivities and makes us genuinely humble. As Dominicans, we see the distinction between "academic" and "pastoral" as a false dichotomy. "Pastoral studies" can be pursued in a critical, reflective, and scholarly fashion. And scholarship — whether biblical, historical, philosophical, or theological — is pastorally aware, guided, and sensitive. The intellectual life does not separate us from other people but is a way of serving people. The scholar too can be both pastor and prophet.

This relates to a second characteristic of Dominican intellectual life, its connectedness to other aspects of our heritage, its ability to see relationships, and its roots in contemplation. We can readily identify our apostolic, missionary, intellectual, artistic, mystical, liturgical, and social traditions. But these traditions, while distinguishable, are not separable. They are interdependent. Is Thomas to be seen as a preacher, a thinker, or a mystic? To separate our intellectual life from its connections and roots is to produce a sterile rationalism. Our intellectual lives cannot be separated from our contemplative lives. Dominican reflection is both pastoral and contemplative, rooted in the world and rooted in prayer, at the service of the people and at the service of God. Both God and the people lie at the heart of the truth that we seek. Our search for truth is prayerful (contemplative), intelligent (using our reason), and practical (pastoral). The *caritas* that we seek to become in our continuing formation is not at odds with the *veritas* that we seek to grasp, or be grasped by, in our being continuing students, life-long learners. Rather, they go hand in hand.

On this feast of St. Thomas, then, we call to mind our search for Truth; our personal and corporate quest to be people of charity; and our priorities of ministry and continuing formation, or proclaiming the truth and living it. We do justice to Thomas not when we repeat his thoughts but when we follow his example. He remains a model for us today.

Your brother, in Truth and with Love,

Don

1. January 28, 1986, Feast of St. Thomas Aquinas

4, Pluralism[1]

Dear Brothers,

We come once again to a significant Dominican feast, that of Saint Catherine of Siena, one of the great women in the history of the Church, a doctor of the Church, an ecclesially conscious, politically courageous, and deeply contemplative woman. As we celebrate this feast, I would like to turn our thoughts in a theological direction and reflect on three issues that affect our lives.

Catherine herself was an apostle to a divided Church; so too in many ways are we. Her capacity to love the Church was equalled only by her capacity to challenge the Church. And she always sought a deepened theological understanding as a source of insight and strength.

The three issues that I have chosen also require theological clarification and reflection. Two of them lie at the source of strong differences among us (the theology of pluralism and the theology of the Church) and the other pertains more to the effect of such differences (the theology of the human person). Our feelings and attitudes toward pluralism, our understanding of the nature of the Church, and our ways of relating to each other are not issues that we can reflect upon once and for all and then they go away. They require continuous dialog and reflection. So I welcome your own theological contributions as well to what must be a continuing dialog.

PLURALISM

What we seek is a theology of pluralism, an understanding of pluralism that is rooted in faith, an appreciation of what it means to believe that God acts and is present in our midst in diverse and even conflicting ways. We need to affirm the value of pluralism in the life of the Church and also be critical of pluralism. Pluralism comes from God, but that does not imply that anything and everything is "of God." Some realities that fall under the umbrella of pluralism may also be an effect of sin.

Let us first acknowledge the value of plurality. The Catholic tradition is and always has been woven together out of diverse cultures, structures, and theologies. Our belief is simply that the transcendent God cannot be revealed adequately in the created order except in diverse and manifold ways. Each human perspective is human and limited but God is unlimited. God has spoken and continues to speak through diversity.

1. April 29, 1986, Feast of St. Catherine of Siena

Any cursory historical study alerts us to the diversity out of which the history of the Church, doctrine, and theology have been woven. This fact is as true of the first century and New Testament Christianity as of every century since. We ought not too quickly attempt a superficial harmonization of the Christianity(ies) that lies underneath our New Testament. The theology of James is quite distinct from that of Paul, and not obviously reconcilable (contrast Galatians 2:15-16 and James 2:14-17). Likewise the organization of the community in Jerusalem under the leadership of James was a contrast to the organization of those communities evangelized by Paul. And the problems they faced differed as well — the problems facing the Jewish Christians in Jerusalem and those facing the Christian communities in Galatia, Thessalonica, Corinth, or Rome.

The theology of the Gospel of Matthew is distinct from that of Paul and from that of James, in some ways not as extreme as either of them. Likewise the organization and life of Matthew's church is distinct, whether it be situated in Antioch or Caesarea or somewhere else. And the Petrine style of leadership was distinct — perhaps sociologically the only style that was able to hold together the diverse Christian experiences and worlds. And none of these (Peter, Paul, James, Matthew, Luke, Mark) reflect the unique theology, problems, and leadership style manifest in that of the Johannine community. Pluralism seems to have been a part of God's intention for the Christian Church from the beginning.

Pluralism also seems to have been a part of our Dominican tradition from quite early on. There is no need to re-trace our history and struggles, but a text from Humbert of the Romans' commentary on the prologue to the Constitutions is illuminating.

We who are under obedience to a single Master are said to live by a single profession. And it is right that we who are united in this way should be found uniform in the observances of our canonical, that is, regular, religious life. It is the general practice among approved religious orders which live by a common profession that they should display the highest degree of uniformity in external things, not only in their observances, but also in their habit, their buildings, and in various other things too. It is with a certain sadness that we must realize how far we differ from the rest on this point. They have their churches and monastic buildings all conforming to the same pattern and arranged in the same way, but we have almost as many different patterns and arrangements of our churches and buildings as we have houses. They are uniform in the colour, shape, size and cost of their clothes; but we are not like that. One man has a black cappa, another a red one, and yet another a grey one. Some people's cappas have a wide opening, some have a very narrow one; some appear very expensive, some are cheap and some are in between. One man has a narrow scapular, another a broad one; some of them have pointed hoods at the back, others do not. Some of them have a long neck opening, some have a short one, and some have folds at the cheeks and some do not. Some people have cappas which cover their whole tunic, while others have cappas improperly shorter than their tunics; some of them are so short that they attract attention, while others are so long that they attract attention. Similarly with scapulars: some are very long, some are very short. And it is the same with the lay brothers: one has one kind of scapular, while another has one totally different in colour and in all the other ways mentioned above.

Other orders also observe uniformity in their shoes. But with us one man has black shoes and another has red shoes; some wear coarse, religious shoes, while others wear worldly, open shoes. Some are fastened one way, some are fastened in quite another way. Some of us have got into the way of wearing shoes so large that they almost come up to the knee, whereas others are very short, and some are in between.

Not only in our buildings and in our habit, but also in some of the customs we follow in the Divine Office and in many other things, there is tremendous diversity between our different provinces and even between different houses in a single province.

The reason for this diversity is the difference between different countries, the equal status of all the provinces and houses, and the excellent minds some people have. Different countries all have had different customs, and out of this diversity different people have brought different things to the Order, even though it is only one Order. And since the houses and provinces are all equal, one province or house is not obliged to follow the customs of any other or to conform itself to any other. And since intelligent brethren are of the opinion that their own customs are as good as anyone else's they are reluctant to abandon them unless an ordination of a General Chapter defines what practice is to be preferred. (From *Early Dominicans, Selected Writings*, edited by Simon Tugwell [New York, NY: Paulist Press, 1982], pp. 141-142.)

Again, conflict, diversity, and pluralism are not "modern" or post-Vatican II facts and experiences.

Diversity is sometimes easy to affirm; the conflict and hostility it almost inevitably creates is not as easy to accept. We prefer harmony, even when that may not be God's immediate intention. I recall a theological insight of Karl Rahner's, that someone may be given the gift to be an accelerator and someone else the gift to be a brake. Is that possible? That the Spirit could be acting in our midst not only in diverse but even conflicting ways? Underneath our theology of pluralism is our theology of the Holy Spirit.

At the same time that we affirm the value and providential character of pluralism, however, we must be ready to be critical. There are dangers inherent in a naive optimism. There are two false approaches to pluralism — neither well grounded theologically. The weakness in a simplistic "conservative" approach is to try to confine plurality too quickly within clearly defined, authoritative, secure limits. Does this do justice to what we know about the Holy Spirit? The weakness in a simplistic "liberal" approach is an excessive tolerance, as if all tolerance is always good. Pure tolerance makes convictions a matter of personal taste. It is an attitude that makes religion purely a personal or private matter. The Dominican commitment to *veritas* can accept neither of these simplistic approaches to pluralism. Neither of them goes deeply enough into the heart of the matter —pneumatology. What does it mean to believe in the Holy Spirit — the principle of both the unity and the diversity in the Catholic experience!

Do I believe that the Holy Spirit is truly at work in our world today? Can the new wine be contained in the old wineskins? Does newness imply no need whatever for the old wineskins? How do I discern what the Holy Spirit is doing at this period of history? Is it possible for the Holy Spirit to be at the source of some of our conflicts? Is the Holy Spirit trying to stretch us in some way? Is it at all possible that the Holy Spirit is at work within someone or some movement that is quite distinct, even in conflict with how I sense the Holy Spirit to be present in my life? What does it mean in the concrete to believe in God as Spirit?

The challenge of pluralism forces us to think through very carefully the theology of the Holy Spirit and the theology of the Church.

THE CHURCH

Pneumatology and ecclesiology are both significant areas of theology that confront us today. What I say here is not new. We have known for some time that ecclesiology lies at the heart of our conflicting perspectives. Ecclesiology was at the center of the work of Vatican II, and the documents of Vatican II themselves contain conflicting ecclesiologies.

We have become accustomed to thinking in terms of models of church, realizing that varied models are not necessarily exclusive. Yet different models imply different ecclesiologies, and different ecclesiologies imply different churches — if we translate theory and theology into practice and life. Thus we ought not be completely surprised to wake up and realize that at least for the past twenty years we have been working for different churches, even for conflicting and competing churches.

There are several ways of describing these conflicting ecclesiologies. One is to contrast an ecclesiology from above and an ecclesiology from below, or the hierarchical church and the popular church, or a clerically dominated church and a laity-oriented church. This way of speaking contains insight and yet is too great a simplification. An either/or way of presenting the contrast does not do justice to the ecclesiologies of the majority of us. Only small numbers in the Province would gravitate more exclusively toward one extreme or the other. Most of us see the Holy Spirit as active in the world and Church *both* "from above" *and* "from below." We do not want to exaggerate a polarization that most of us do not accept. Nor do we want to deny naively deep differences among us.

A deep-seated conflict in the Province — as in the Church — is the interpretation of Vatican II. It is not at all a question of some being pre-Vatican II and others post-Vatican II. The conflict is over two (or more) competing interpretations of Vatican II — a question of the hermeneutics of Vatican II. Whose understanding or interpretation will prevail? I would describe these two interpretations as follows, and both have bases in the conciliar documents: those for whom the hierarchical and institutional side of the Church is primary, although not to the exclusion of other aspects of the Church; and those for whom the hierarchical and institutional side of the Church is significant but secondary. How one interprets Vatican II is closely related to what type of Church we are working for.

Two things seem almost self-evident. (1) What interpretation of Vatican II eventually becomes authoritative rests with history and is probably not something most of us will live long enough to know. This has been true of most Councils. They created as many questions as they solved. What would eventually become the authoritative interpretation of Nicea or Chalcedon took the following centuries to work out. Thus most of us will live our lives in the midst of these conflicting ecclesiologies. (2) The conflicts during the next twenty years will not be less painful than during the previous twenty. If anything, they will be more. Given the issues of the theology of priesthood, the relationship of the church to world and religion to politics, the laity and the Scriptures, liberation theology, the role of women, the tension between a Eurocentric and world church, not to mention many other issues, conflict within the Church is not likely to decrease.

Our contribution can be to live through and work through these potentially divisive questions *as brothers*. None of us knows the ultimate outcome. Each of us has been given the gift of the Spirit. Each of us has some contribution to make. We need not evasively cover over our differences. We need only affirm our brotherhood as a bond that frees us to struggle together. We have the freedom to discuss together — knowing that agreement is not our expectation, and that respect for each brother is his right.

THE DIGNITY OF THE HUMAN PERSON

Pluralism does not imply that anything goes, that every opinion has equal claim to validity. And a critique of pluralism does not imply that my perspective is the normative one, and that the limits be set by how far the diversity deviates from my norm. Pluralism, in the concrete circumstances of our lives, raises another theological issue besides that of the Holy Spirit, this time an anthropological one, our theology of the human person. Perhaps nothing challenges the practice of our faith more than the attitude we sustain toward those who deeply disagree with us. Yet, practically speaking, what does it mean to say we believe that every human person is created to be an image or likeness of God? Whether woman or man, right or left, gay or straight, old or young, learned or less educated, and on and on.

It is always a great personal challenge to see our brothers and sisters as "icons of God." Such dignity deserves great respect. We must appreciate both the dignity and the imperfection that comes from being human and realize that what is most important about each of us we all have in common — that we are "in Christ."

I think of an older man in the Province for whom fraternal love and human dignity implies that we not treat him as if he were finished, having nothing more to offer. What does it mean to realize that someone has given forty years of his life to the service of the Church? I think of a middle-aged man in the Province whose political views are strongly to the left, and how that deeply held political conviction prevents many from seeing in him a man of great faith, hope, with a deep capacity for love. What does it mean to embrace as brother someone who threatens us because of the clarity of his option for solidarity with the poor? I am thinking of a man who told me the other day that he was gay, a man in religious life long before I joined the Order. I feel that his human dignity and self-worth have been eroded through the years and wonder when we will talk more comfortably about questions of sexuality such as these. I look around the Province at my brothers and I see fragile, talented, vulnerable, hard-working, flawed, dedicated, hurting, self-sacrificing men. We come in many shapes and sizes, protecting ourselves and yet yearning to be connected with each other — each an image of our wonderful God.

Pluralism cannot get in the way of our recognizing the beauty and dignity of each individual among us. To become brothers does not mean superficially glossing over deeply felt differences either.

I have not written about these questions to provide answers but to provoke discussion and promote dialog. Do you believe in the Holy Spirit? What is your understanding of Church to which you are giving your life? Do you see in your brothers the image of Jesus Christ? These are the questions that both divide and unite us.

As we celebrate this feast of our sister Catherine, I ask that we continue to discuss and reflect together on our theological understanding of the Holy Spirit, the Church, and the human person, and on the implications of those reflections for our common life.

Your brother in Dominic and Catherine,
Don

Catherine of Siena "ecclesially conscious, politically courageous and deeply contemplative woman."
(p. 27)

Artist:
Placid Stuckenschneider, OSB

5, Obedience[1]

Dear Brothers,

One year ago, for the feast of St. Dominic, my first letter to the Province was on the subject of preaching — preaching as an apostolic priority in the Province, as a norm for evaluating all our apostolic activities within the Province, as the mission in the context of which our Dominican vocation takes on its coherence. This year I would like to address another topic close to the heart and vision of Dominic: obedience.

One of the most powerful biblical images is that of "the servant of the Lord" — the one who does the will of the Lord. True obedience and servanthood are practically synonymous.

A biblical theology of obedience and servanthood makes two points quite clear. (1) The foundation of the servant's life is God. A servant is first of all a servant of God. Radical obedience is always to God. (2) Servanthood not only implies obedience, but also frequently implies suffering, often the pain of rejection. The suffering is not because God wants it, but because there is no way to do what God is asking without embracing the specific pain it may involve. God did not love Jeremiah less because what he asked Jeremiah to endure was more. There was no way in which Jeremiah could have done God's will, spoken God's word, to those people in that period of history without opening himself to the pain his particular vocation or mission would entail. Whatever else may be said about obedience, this biblical image of the servant must be the cornerstone of our understanding.

OBEDIENCE AS LISTENING

Obedience is primarily concerned with our relationship to God, and it calls us into a posture of listening to God, of becoming "hearers of the Word" before we become "proclaimers of the Word," and thus establishes an integral relationship between obedience, contemplation, and the apostolic life of the Preacher.

Obedience, etymologically, comes from the Latin *oboedire*, or *ob*, a preposition implying something relational, and *audire*, a verb meaning to hear or to listen. We must listen before we can truly hear, and we must hear before we can genuinely respond. The obediential posture is that of a listener. We should as brothers bound together by the vow of obedience certainly examine ourselves and ask: What is the quality of my listening?

1. August 8, 1986, Feast of St. Dominic

the extent of my capacity to listen?

We first of all, of course, listen to God. But God's will or word is most often mediated. And therefore we also ask to what else or to whom else do we listen.

We listen to the Church, in its teaching and its liturgy. We listen to the world, as we attempt to read or hear "the signs of the times," the cry of the poor. We listen to ourselves — our best selves, true selves, not our sinful or selfish selves. And we listen to others — to friends, to those to whom we minister, to those most in need in our society, and to our brothers and sisters in the faith, especially our brothers and sisters in Dominic. It is this latter listening which draws us close to a particular Dominican form of obedience. Listening is a contemplative act: we listen to the Word. It is also a fraternal or communal act: we listen to each other.

OBEDIENCE AND COMMUNITY

Although obedience implies a profound relationship with the Living God, and the contemplative's capacity to listen to both God and world, the most concrete effect of a freely chosen, vowed obedience for us as Dominicans is the community, life together. This is where the vow of obedience is most often experienced and where it is found the most challenging. For over and above the virtue of obedience which affects all Christians, the vow binds us together as brothers, no longer seemingly autonomous centers of activity but rather interdependent lives lived together. Through the vow of obedience we have chosen to allow brothers or sisters a place, a space, a role in our lives. We have a special obligation to hear and listen to them, when they speak individually, and even more so when they speak corporately.

Pierre Raffin makes the point that it is the fraternal dimension of obedience which is the hallmark of the mendicants in contrast to an earlier monastic understanding of obedience, or even the later Ignatian understanding. Obedience among Dominicans implies community life and vice versa. First of all, we owe obedience to one another. We have obliged ourselves to listen to each other. Religious profession binds us to one another: this is the first concrete realization of what Dominican obedience implies. As Raffin writes, "Dominican obedience is based on a radical trust in people. The dependence upon one another, which we accept by making profession in the Order, presupposes that we trust one another, that we trust in the personal uprightness and prudence of our brothers." (*"L'obéissance dominicaine", La Vie Spirituelle* [Jan-Feb, 1985], 39-50.)

Another quality of Dominican obedience, highlighted by Herbert McCabe ("Obedience", *New Blackfriars* [June, 1984], 280-288), is that obedience is more a question of intelligence than of will, of a mutuality of learning than a simple doing, and thus again that it is something which takes place in common or in a community of brothers and sisters. For Thomas Aquinas, the act of commanding is not primarily an act of the will but of the intelligence, the act of one who understands what is to be done. McCabe draws out the implications of this:

> In our tradition on the other hand, which sees obedience as a kind of learning process, a matter of practical intelligence, obedience is something that brings people to share a common mind. For our tradition it matters that the superior should be right. S/he too has to learn, to be obedient. For the modern style an obedient house is one in which the will of the superior prevails over that of the subject. For our tradition an obedient house is one which has got as near as possible to the truth, in which there is general agreement about what is to be done, so that the will of the superior hardly enters into it. The job of the superior is not to make her or his will prevail, it is to play the central role in an educational process by which the good for the house becomes clear to everyone... Obedience, then, for us is not simply a matter of efficiency in getting something done but of fraternal unity, and it would perhaps be better if instead of speaking of a vow of obedience we spoke of a vow of solidarity.

This vow of solidarity with the community helps us understand the role of the community meeting and a house chapter in our lives, as well as a provincial or general chapter. It is in these corporate gatherings that the challenge of Dominican obedience will make itself felt. But this takes us to another level at which the fraternal character of Dominican obedience is experienced — the role of leadership in a Dominican community.

OBEDIENCE AND LEADERSHIP

Obedience involves our fidelity to God, to ourselves, to others, and Dominican obedience involves in particular a fidelity to our Dominican brothers and sisters and our Dominican vocation. But this relationship to our fellow Dominicans, whether in a local community or in the Province, also involves the relationship between leadership and membership. This relationship, to which unfortunately we can jump too quickly when discussing obedience, is not the starting point for understanding either the virtue or the vow. Inevitably, however, it is a relationship which must also be addressed. And in doing so we must remember, following upon what has already been said, that obedience calls both membership and leadership to responsibility within community life.

Dominican obedience is communal fraternal in character. It is inseparable from our Dominican form of government in which authority is derived from the community which expresses itself through general, provincial, or house chapters. Authority itself is both limited and obligated by constitutions and capitular, corporate decisions. The chapter at all levels plays a central role in Dominican life.

Yet I frankly admit that the effort to correlate the needs and desires of the individual members and the corporate decisions and needs of the Province as a whole is a most difficult and delicate task. The question is: what content does the Dominican vow of obedience have for us? Is the vow effective? Does it strengthen our vocation and mission? It is one of the hinges that holds us together. If it is missing, or not working, we fall off in all directions. Thus we fail to exercise a corporate ministry; nor do we have a corporate impact on the life of the Church.

Part of our difficulty, I believe, is that we have been oscillating back and forth for the past twenty years between two models of obedience, neither properly Dominican! The first, seemingly more traditional model, overly simplified, runs something like this. Provincial leadership takes the initiative; the individual is consulted in the process; the provincial makes the decision. The second model, explicitly operative since the early 1970s at least, placed more responsibility on the individual. The individual member took his own initiative; provincial leadership was often consulted in the process; but the individual was the final, determinative factor.

Each model had advantages and disadvantages. But neither took into sufficient account the fraternal character of Dominican obedience, the first by placing the responsibility primarily on leadership, and the second by placing it primarily on membership, whereas Dominican obedience is always collaboration between the two, *a reciprocal and mutual process of learning.* The first, seemingly more traditional model lent itself to authoritarianism and a lack of concern for how the Holy Spirit was acting within an individual. It collapsed in our contemporary, rapidly changing, cultural situation. There have been sufficient critiques of "blind obedience" and the abuses of civil and ecclesiastical power to which it is open.

But the second, more recent model had disadvantages as well. It did not form and support corporate commitments, decisions, or responsibilities. Leadership lost any capacity to lead or implement corporate goals and policies. Thus corporate and capitular decisions or goals remained ineffective. The corporate good and corporate life were undermined. Any corporate or provincial or communal planning became a precarious and futile venture, resting on nothing more than the hoped-for good will of those who were so inclined.

There is, however, a model between these two which I propose. Dominican obedience implies that both leadership and membership profess and practice obedience. There must be a mutuality of fraternal listening. The initiative can be taken by either membership or leadership. What is initiated is a process of discernment and decision-making in which both the individual brother and leadership (or a particular community) are integrally involved. Our obedience is never a question of "the provincial gets his way," or "the individual brother gets his way." Obedience does not set us over against each other like that, but rather implies that we as brothers are committed to a common process. If there is no process, no discernment, or if the individual is not fully respected, or if the provincial leadership is not integrally involved, then there is no obedience to speak of no matter what else may be going on.

Someone may suggest that the word discernment is not a Dominican word. Yet it is, and we need to retrieve it in its fully Dominican sense. Both Eckhart and Tauler speak of discernment and it occupies a central place in the theology of Catherine, for whom it is one of the three fundamental virtues (humility, charity, and discernment). Or perhaps we would prefer to use a way of speaking more akin to Thomas. Then we can talk about the virtue of prudence, and discernment or obedience as a process of coming to a corporate prudential judgment.

But, in Dominican obedience, there is a final step, after the mutual listening, after the fraternal dialogue, after communal discernment. All that is trust in people. Then comes the trust in the brotherhood and its corporate processes, the chapters. This allows the closure of the process. It is the function of leadership to see that things move: the decisions of the provincial chapter, responses to requests and needs, calls from the larger Church, intervention when proper responsibility and initiative are not in fact forthcoming at the local or individual level. In the process both leadership and membership will have learned, grown, perhaps been stretched, and in decision-making, leadership can effectively serve the common good.

The difficult but important challenge of Dominican leadership is how to bring together the needs of the individual and the needs of the community or province, and also how to bring these together with the needs of our world. I have several times been impressed by Frederick Buechner's definition of vocation which relates closely to my understanding of obedience. He writes:

> Vocation comes from the Latin *vocare*, to call, and means the work a man is called to by God.
>
> There are all different kinds of voices calling you to all different kinds of work, and the problem is to find out which is the voice of God rather than of Society, say, or the Superego, or Self-Interest.
>
> By and large a good rule for finding out is this. The kind of work God usually calls you to is the kind of work (a) that you need most to do and (b) that the world most needs to have done. If you really get a kick out of your work, you've presumably met requirement (a), but if your work is writing TV deodorant commercials, the chances are you've missed requirement (b). On the other hand, if your work is being a doctor in a leper colony, you have probably met requirement (b), but if most of the time you're bored and depressed by it, the chances are you have not only bypassed (a) but probably aren't helping your patients much either.
>
> Neither the hair shirt nor the soft berth will do. The place God calls you to is the place where your deep gladness and the world's deep hunger meet. (*The Alphabet of Grace* [New York: Harper and Row, 1985], 95.)

This is the challenge of obedience for Dominican leadership, how to facilitate a coming together of the individual member's deep gladness and the Province's mission and the world's deep hunger. The process ultimately depends upon a freely chosen gift of the self to the brotherhood — the spirit of collaboration and sense of fraternity.

Dominican obedience implies the trust that Pierre Raffin spoke of. Michael Downey writes of Jean Vanier, "A true leader is one who has the extraordinary ability to call forth from others the very best they have to give" and "The proper use of authority aims at bringing about balance between the importance of ideals and the importance of the people who pursue them" (*A Blessed Weakness, The Spirit of Jean Vanier and l'Arche* [San Francisco: Harper and Row, 1986], 37 and 69). Leadership and membership, the individual good and the corporate good, are not to be defined over against each other but in relationship to each other.

OBEDIENCE AND POWER

One of the constructive aspects of the vow of obedience is that it makes us confront our use of power, just as the vow of chastity challenges us to face the use of our human sexuality, and as the vow of poverty confronts our relationship to materiality, material goods and comforts. Sexuality, material goods, and power are very human elements in our lives, and how the vows enable us to live with them as people of the gospel is not something to take lightly.

Christian chastity teaches us that human sexuality is good, but that it is distorted when it becomes too dominant a source or motive in our lives. The truly chaste person is one who is truly sexual but who freely puts that sexuality at the service of the Lord. Christian poverty (the virtue, of course, and the vow, not the economic condition) teaches us that material goods are indeed good, and yet we can distort them when we view them as possessions or are dominated by our desire for them, unable to share and distribute them equitably. A truly poor person in the religious sense is one who enjoys and can delight in material goods as God's gifts but freely puts them at the service of the gospel. Likewise, Christian obedience teaches us that power is good; yet power is distorted when it defines us over against others or above others, when it dominates our ambitions or desires. The truly obedient person is one who sees that power too is good but has learned to use power for the sake of the reign of God.

We deal here with significant human realities and yet we are fragile creatures. How much all of us want to be in control — of our lives, our relationships, our apostolates, and even our relationship with God. Our socialization has geared us to seek independence rather than interdependence. We live under the fallacy of self-sufficiency. This is why obedience lies at the heart of our spiritual lives and struggles. To hold power as a force for good and yet to be able to let go is the sign of a truly free and spiritual person.

The vows teach us to be discriminating. Not all power is the same. So often we think of power as coercion: I can get whatever I want if I have the power. But this is not the kind of power which God longs for us to have, the power of which the Scriptures speak, the power of the Spirit and the power of love. The kind of power that the person of obedience seeks is the kind of power only God can give. True power does not imply the ability to have my way but rather the freedom not to have my way. Power is not something that I posses by myself, but something that we share in common. This is what Christian obedience and our vow is all about. Rollo May distinguished five kinds of power: exploitative, manipulative, competitive, nutrient, and integrative. (*Power and Innocence*, [New York: W W Norton and Co., 1972].) We could each well ask — whether as leadership or membership — which kind of power most characterizes my style of life and approach to others.

So much more could be said, but I have only wanted to invite us into a reflection on Dominican obedience as we prepare to celebrate the feast of our brother Dominic.

From the beginning of the Order, St. Dominic required the brethren to promise him community and obedience. He himself humbly submitted to the decisions, especially the laws, which, after full deliberation, the general chapter of the brethren established. But outside the general chapter, he required — kindly but firmly indeed — voluntary obedience from all to the commands which, after due deliberation, he gave while governing the Order. A community, indeed, to remain faithful to its spirit and its mission, needs a principle of unity, which it obtains through obedience (The Book of the Constitutions of the Dominican Order 17, I).

Your brother in Dominic,
Don

"These images speak to us of the dream
that captured us in the beginning." (p. 127).

Dominic, by Mary Ansgar, OP,
after a wooden sculpture at Segovia, Spain.

6, The Option for Solidarity with the Poor[1]

Dear Brothers,

In the third draft of their pastoral letter on economic justice, the United States bishops continue to place the fundamental option for the poor at the center of their teaching (see paragraphs 84-94).

"The obligation to provide justice for all means that the poor have the single most urgent claim on the conscience of the nation" (85). "As individuals and as a nation, therefore, we are called to make a fundamental 'option for the poor'"(86). "The fulfillment of the basic needs of the poor is of the highest priority" (89). The bishops continue to challenge us toward "a new American experiment" within the economic life of the nation (paragraphs 291-321).

The United States bishops in their roles as preachers and teachers have set for us a profound and challenging example. May we as Preachers prove to be ready to take up the challenge and follow their lead.

Taking up the challenge flows readily from our Dominican tradition and the priority it has given to the cry of the poor. Names like Dominic, Albert, Catherine, Francisco de Vitoria, Bartolomé de las Casas, Martin de Porres, Rose of Lima, Henri Dominic Lacordaire, and Louis-Joseph Lebret come immediately to mind.

As we celebrate once again the feast of our brother Albert, and as we have just recently celebrated the feast of our brother Martin de Porres, I would like to call our attention to the option for solidarity with the poor.

What does this way of speaking imply? What are its implications for our apostolates? For our common life?

THE OPTION FOR SOLIDARITY WITH THE POOR

The conscious option for solidarity with the poor does not imply a rejection of ministry to the middle class or even the wealthy. It does place definite requirements upon such ministry, however. Such a ministry must be globally conscious and socially responsible. Although the option for the poor does not mean ministry exclusively to the economically poor and socially marginal or vulnerable, it still implies a preference given to ministry to the poor.

The expression, "preferential option for the poor," or variations of it, is *not* univocal. Such an expression will not have the same implications

1. November 15, 1986, Feast of St. Albert the Great

for each and every one of us. What it requires of one brother may vary from what it requires of another. What it requires of all of us, however, is that our preaching and ministry be socio-ethically responsible, that we ourselves become more socially and politically educated, and that we become aware that our faith and discipleship do have political and public implications.

"Solidarity with the poor" is rather an enticement, an invitation, a conscience prodder, consciousness-raising language, a highly tensive language rich with implications, hence a means of conscientization or conversion, or personal conversion to a social consciousness, a social conversion. It draws us into unrest with our present way of living or previous content in preaching. It makes us more conscious, more restless, more challenged.

"Solidarity with the poor" also requires that we approach every question, every issue from the perspective of a social consciousness. Our common life and our ministries cannot be divorced from the social questions of our day. This does not mean that we approach every issue exclusively and only from a social perspective, but that the social, political, and economic aspects of an issue be a constant factor in our awareness. Such an awareness makes social justice a mission to which we are all called within our varying apostolates.

"Solidarity with the poor" is a process. It takes time. It is not something accomplished within us overnight. It involves personal transformation as well as a commitment to social transformation. Solidarity is always pulling us and pushing us one step further.

Taking up the challenge from Rose of Lima (p. 42)

Artist, MARY ANSGAR, OP

We may be led where we would rather not go (Jn 21:18). Albert Nolan made this point well in a talk he gave in London in 1984, in which he elucidated solidarity with the poor by reference to our traditional approach to spiritual growth.

In their third draft of the pastoral, the bishops speak about the option for the poor in the language of "fundamental option" (86). A fundamental option is not optional, however. It is not something we take or leave. It is, morally speaking, the only choice we have. And it is a choice that is then foundational, at the basis of everything else we do. The option for solidarity is a decision we make about how to live our lives.

The option for the poor is ultimately not for the poor alone, but choosing to be for humankind. It is an option for the gospel, the whole gospel, and nothing but the gospel. "Action on behalf of justice and participation in the transformation of the world fully appear to us as a constitutive dimension of the preaching of the gospel" ("Justice in the World," 1971 Synod of Bishops, in *Vatican Collection,* vol 2, *More Postconciliar Documents,* ed. Austin Flannery, OP, p. 696.).

How this option for solidarity will work itself out in the concrete in my life I can never know in advance. As I said, the expression is not univocal, but an enticement. I must give myself to it and see where God leads me. We all ought to accept humbly the fact that we do not know precisely what the implications of this option may be for us as individuals or as a Province. But we ought not be afraid or hesitant. Together we can move both wisely and courageously in this direction to which the gospel calls us, the "signs of the times" impel us, and with which the bishops challenge all Catholics and United States citizens.

We ought humbly accept the fact that none of us is perfect or "has arrived" with respect to this solidarity. None of us can say, "You want to know what the option for the poor means? Look at me." Rather this is something with which each of us must wrestle. But there can be no backing away from the decision. So let us begin to explore together what this means for us. Let us begin to talk to our friends about it. Let us talk to our brothers and sisters in the Dominican family. Let us begin to talk about it as communities.

I must raise these questions myself in terms of my own spiritual life, my own preaching and teaching, my work as Provincial. Last year in Bolivia, I paid 1,500,000 pesos for three candy bars. Bolivia is considered one of the poorest countries in the Western Hemisphere. How can I help our country to move in an economic direction that does not promote and perpetuate such global poverty? Last year in San Salvador I could see and feel the effects of that government's tactics of terror. What is my response to the growing number of refugees from Central America? Where do I stand? Last year a Czechoslovakian woman, a member of the Dominican laity there, sought out the opportunity to talk to me about the lack of religious freedom in her country. How can we avoid being naive about repression in Eastern Europe? Our option for solidarity will raise these questions and many more, but we cannot stand back from pursuing them with cowardly excuses that we are not economists or not knowledgeable in these matters. When have Dominicans ever used ignorance as their excuse? When have we ever taken refuge in a lack of education? Our tradition of learning demands that we learn about these matters and discuss them in the light of the gospel.

SOME IMPLICATIONS

Although the implications of this option for the poor remain to be worked out by us in the coming years, some suggestions or questions can be posed.

A fundamental option for solidarity with the poor has particular implications or obligations for those of us who have chosen to live the common life. Which is more apparent in my life, the influence of evangelical simplicity or United States consumerism? Solidarity with the poor implies a freely chosen self-limitation with respect to goods and comforts in the face of our society's consumerism.

We must continually call to mind the integral relationship between what we practice and what we preach, between our living the gospel and how we proclaim the gospel. Paul VI, in his apostolic exhortation on evangelization, *Evangelii Nuntiandi*, puts it well. "These 'signs of the times' should find us vigilant. Either tacitly or aloud — but always forcefully — we are being asked: Do you really believe what you are proclaiming? Do you live what you believe? Do you really preach what you live? The witness of life has become more than ever an essential condition for real effectiveness in preaching" (76).

When the final draft of the bishops' pastoral has been approved, how will I preach solidarity with the poor?

What one decision will I make about my life personally and what one decision can we make as a community that will reflect our decision to be in solidarity with the poor?

How can I place myself in some situations that will give me a more concrete feel for the effects of poverty?

With whom am I going to discuss this further so as to come to a wise and resolute decision about this step to which we as United States Catholics are being called?

The principle of solidarity with the poor has apostolic and pastoral implications as well. Whatever I do, wherever I minister, how will this solidarity affect my ministry?

As we plan new ministries or expand ministry within the Province, how can our ministry be increasingly with the poor and among the poor?

I am not suggesting that the above are the most important questions for us to ask, but only that the option of solidarity must have some concrete implications for us. Together we must raise those questions and together we must respond to them.

In our human and spiritual adult lives, there are three significant and difficult struggles. We may want to relate them to the classic struggles with the devil, the flesh, and the world, or to the norms of obedience, chastity, and poverty, but whether we do so or not all of us has to face the struggle with our own ego and the self, the struggle for intimacy and relationship, and the struggle for justice and peace on earth. Our relationship with God and our desire for holiness requires that we not back away from any of them. In our continuing renewal, I hope we can enter into these struggles together as brothers and with our sisters. The "preferential option for the poor" invites us to undertake a search that we as people of the gospel cannot ignore.

Solidarity with the poor will not be easy. We are just beginning to explore something of what it means. As a closing reflection, we can take the closing lines of the poem, "Return" (1980) by Carolyn Forche. [From *The Country Between Us*, New York, Harper and Row, 1981.]

Her subject is El Salvador. She writes upon her return to the United States.

> And so, you say, you've learned a little
> about starvation: a child like a supper scrap
> filling with worms, many children strung
> together, as if they were cut from paper
> and all in a delicate chain. And that people
> who rescue physicists, lawyers and poets
> lie in their beds at night with reports
> of mice introduced into women, of men
> whose testicles are crushed like eggs.
> That they cup their own parts
> with their bedsheets and move themselves
> slowly, imagining bracelets affixing
> their wrists to a wall where the naked
> are pinned, where the naked are tied open
> and left to the hands of those who erase
> what they touch. We are all erased

by them, and no longer resemble decent
men. We no longer have the hearts,
the strength, the lives of women.
Your problem is not your life as it is
in America, not that your hands, as you
tell me, are tied to do something. It is
that you were born to an island of greed
and grace where you have this sense
of yourself as apart from others. It is
not your right to feel powerless. Better
people than you were powerless.
You have not returned to your country,
but to a life you never left.

In solidarity with the poor, and in solidarity with Jesus Christ,
Don

Taking up the challenge
from John Macias
p. 42

Artist, Mary Ansgar, OP

7, Contemplation and Prayer[1]

Dear Brothers,

As we celebrate the feast of Catherine of Siena, I am very aware that the challenge issued to us by Pope John XXIII and the Second Vatican Council has not yet been accomplished, namely, the ongoing renewal of religious life. This task is of utmost importance, for on it everything else depends. It is imperative that we continue to renew ourselves, deepen our love for Jesus Christ and the gospel, and not back off from the continuous giving of ourselves to the spiritual life. In our continuing and constructive efforts toward renewal, the contemplative side of our lives has suffered from lack of attention. We must accept, as Preachers, that we are also contemplatives. We are both contemplatives and apostles, and neither of these takes precedence over the other. What better topic is there upon which to reflect as we celebrate the feast of Catherine?

What is your own understanding of contemplation? What are those things which foster or nourish your contemplative life? Why does our spirituality of the Word and spirituality of preaching require contemplation?

Perhaps I ought not say "contemplation" but rather "contemplative experience." For it is the experience of the Living God that contemplation both seeks and nourishes. That experience of God makes our faith a living faith. And only a living faith can truly give life to those to whom we are sent.

WHAT IS CONTEMPLATION?

Contemplation is an experiential love of God, the experience both of loving God and of being loved intimately by God. Contemplation helps to distinguish the one who knows a lot about God from the one who has met God. And the people of God are looking for religious who have met God.

Contemplative prayer is a relationship with God that is beyond reflection, and beyond affection, although both reflective prayer or meditation and affective prayer or the prayer of the heart prepare the way for contemplation. Although contemplation and the spiritual life are multi-faceted realities about which much has been written, there are four supports for the contemplative life that I would like to emphasize: discipline, silence, devotion, and Scripture.

1. April 29, 1987, Feast of St. Catherine of Siena

PRAYER AND DISCIPLINE.

The foundational experience in the life of a religious is one's experience of God, and the foundation of one's apostolic life is one's image of God. One's image and experience of God are shaped by prayer, ministry, community, friendships, and one's self-concept. But of these, nothing is more important than prayer.

As individuals and as communities, we need to stand back from time to time and take a look at our commitment to prayer and the Eucharist — at least if we intend to take renewal and attentiveness to spiritual life seriously.

Can I say that there is nothing more important in my life than prayer? As communities can we say that there is nothing more important to us than our common prayer? There may be other things of equal value, but nothing is of greater value than consciously attending to my friendship with God.

This is why I place emphasis on the annual retreat (The Book of the Constitutions of the Order n. 68). There is simply no substitute for it. This is why we place emphasis on a common celebration of the Eucharist. We do not expect a friendship with someone to grow if we do not take time to be with that person. The same is true of friendship with God. We would mistrust any friend who said, "I love you, but I don't have the need to spend any time with you." Growth in prayer requires times of heightened consciousness and attentiveness.

Attentiveness to personal prayer and common prayer require a disciplined life. One of the most difficult things in any commitment is perseverance in the ongoing daily self-giving to the tasks at hand. At this level the consolation, excitement, and romance are put to the test. Only a continual giving of ourselves to prayer will allow our relationship with God to bear fruit. So much spiritual life ceases because we stop nourishing it, somewhere after novitiate, or final profession, or the first years of ministry. Other things become more exciting. But we are the ones who suffer the consequences — as well as those with whom we live, those to whom we minister, and the Church as a whole.

There are legitimate individual differences when it comes to discipline, prayer, Eucharist, and the spiritual life. All of us have our own rhythms of prayer and our own ways of praying. But such differences do not negate the necessity of discipline, prayer, and attentiveness to spiritual growth. Tennyson's King Arthur came to realize the power of prayer.

And slowly answer'd Arthur from the barge;
"The old order changeth, yielding place to new,
And God fulfils himself in many ways,
Lest one good custom should corrupt the world.
Comfort thyself; what comfort is in me?
I have lived my life, and that which I have done
May He within himself make pure! but thou,
If thou shouldst never see my face again,
Pray for my soul. More things are wrought by prayer
this world dreams of. Wherefore, let thy voice
Rise like a fountain for me night and day.
For what are men better than sheep or goats
That nourish a blind life within the brain,
If, knowing God, they lift not hands of prayer
Both for themselves and those who call them friend?"
(from Alfred Lord Tennyson, *The Passing of Arthur, Idylls of the King*)

SILENCE

If we speak about practices which undergird prayer and contemplation, there is none more important than the practice of silence. Yet, if there is a practice which we have almost lost since Vatican II, it has been that of formal silence. Silence is conducive to the spiritual life and contemplative spirit of both the individual and the community.

Contemplation is silence in the presence of God, a consciousness of the divine presence in which my only desire is to be there in God's presence. Neither thoughts, words, or affections convey the reality of the presence. Only silence can express the longing for solidarity with God. To have practiced silence is to be better prepared for encounter with God.

This is not only true in our times of solitude and personal prayer, but also for a community and in common prayer. The times of silence in our common liturgical prayer are precious moments of grace integral to the prayer itself. It reminds us that prayer is not words but presence — to each other and to God. We may well be most one with God when in silence with each other.

This emphasis on silence in no way diminishes the importance of direct communication with each other in our lives together. But there is a rhythm, a time for speech and a time for silence (Eccl. 3:7). Dietrich Bonhoeffer put it: "Let him who cannot be alone beware of community.

Let him who is not in community beware of being alone" (from *Life Together*).

Community silence ought not be something a community experiences only during prayer. There ought to be times and places of silence within the community. The chapel is certainly a place for quiet, as is one's own room. But there should also be set times. These are not artificial or ascetic or romantic, but create a climate, a consciousness, a sense of ourselves as contemplative. This will be something difficult to re-integrate into our common life in a wholesome way, but we should give some thought to it — silence after a certain hour in the evening, or in the morning until a certain hour, or at one meal a week.

There is a long, reliable, theological tradition behind the value of silence, going back as far as the origins of monasticism and to Jesus himself. It will benefit us not to lose it.

MARY AND DEVOTION

One of the modern dangers for religious, since the Reformation and the Enlightenment, and especially in the United States with our separation of church and state, has been the privatizing of religion and our faith. Society prefers to make religion a matter of opinion rather than a question of truth. Only recently are we beginning to rediscover and recognize the public character and social responsibility and political implications of our Catholic faith. We still search out how to express this wisely and courageously. This is one of the great moral challenges for us as Catholic citizens.

At the same time that we begin to assert the public, social, political, and economic implications of our faith as well as its corporate or communal character, we ought not dismiss the importance of the personal, individual, or devotional aspects as well. Corporate or public responsibility and personal or interior growth need not be exclusive of each other nor harmful to each other. The person with a public and socially conscious faith can also be a person of great personal devotion. Indeed, we all ought be both. It is not a question of a choice.

I call our attention to the life of personal devotion since it can be an embarrassment for us, something we don't let on as having or needing, something that we still keep private in an age of public witness, yet something that needs to be acknowledged and supported. I realize that this aspect of our Christian lives is quite personal, often intimate, and not something for publicity, any more than other personal aspects of our lives may be. Yet we ought not be ashamed to say we do have personal devotion in our lives as well as public expressions of our faith, both liturgical and political. We ought not be ashamed because personal devotion is again one of the major supports for the contemplative life, and we are contemplative people. Contemplatives in the world and in ministry and in the public forum, but contemplatives nevertheless.

We ought acknowledge the particular value of devotion to Mary — not an exaggerated devotion, not a devotion unaware of the contemporary theology of Mary, not a devotion that is ecumenically offensive or a devotion that promotes a false image of woman for the modern world, but nevertheless prayer to Mary: a woman of courage, faith, fidelity, and true obedience, a woman full of grace. We do not want to lose our sense of the contemplative, our love of silence, and our capacity to turn to Mary in prayer. We can well bring to her our petition for the conversion of the United States to economic justice at the same time that we are working out the implications of our own option for solidarity with the poor. Mary's *Magnificat* expresses beautifully the prayer of the *anawim*.

THE WORD OF GOD, JUSTICE AND CONTEMPLATION

The heart of Dominican spirituality is the Word of God. It is in the reciprocity between proclaiming the Word and contemplating the Word that Dominican speech takes shape. Our contemplation is affected by our being proclaimers of the Word and our proclamation is affected by our being contemplatives before the Word.

And thus the Scriptures play a foundational role in our lives. The Scriptures are one of Dominic's loves. It would be difficult to know which to emphasize more as a preparation for contemplation, silence or the Scriptures. Both are necessary. We are called upon not only to study the Scriptures, exegete the Scriptures, reflect on the texts of Scripture, but also pray with the Scriptures. Study and prayer are not opposed in the rhythm of Dominican life. They mutually nourish each other, a time for study, a time for prayer. Praying with the Scriptures, studying the Scriptures, and opening the meaning of the Scriptures for others are all part of Dominican contemplation.

We are all preachers, in varied ways. But more important we are Preachers. This latter says something about us whether we are preachers with a small "p" or not. Our spirituality and identity are formed by the Word. We love the Word. We have given our lives to the Word. We are nourished by the Word. We share the Word. We live the Word.

There are many who are not Dominicans who are preachers. The bishops are preachers. But none of them are necessarily Preachers.

"The Word brings us to the foot of the cross,
which we both contemplate and proclaim."
(p. 54).

Artist, ALBERT CARPENTIER, OP

Preaching is the basis of our identity in the Dominican Family, preaching is our mission, and preaching is one of the major sources of our spiritual direction and prayer. Contemplation then does not take us away from the world, but draws us even more deeply into the heart of the world, into the anguish and despair and pain of the world as well as the hopes and joys of the world. This is true because our contemplation is so integrally related to our being Preachers and vice versa. It is the Word that achieves this integration. The Word makes us contemplative preachers and preaching contemplatives. The Word brings us to the foot of the cross which we both contemplate and proclaim.

The cross, which so concisely and symbolically speaks of the mission of Jesus, which is a summary of the whole history of human suffering and victimization, which is a sign of God's unqualified love for humankind, which draws us into the meaning of the resurrection, which remains always something of an enigma before us and challenges us like a parable, this selfsame cross shouts from within us the need to be proclaimed, as a sign of contradiction, as the sign of Jonah, as God's "No" to the history of injustice, as God's judgment on our evil, as the prophetic martyrdom of the Just One. The history of prophecy comes back to haunt us. The cross refuses to let us set it aside. We find ourselves both judged and loved. We humbly proclaim the Word that God called us to contemplate. The words of Micah wring forth, "What I ask of you now is simply this, to act justly, to love tenderly, and to walk humbly with your God" (Micah 6:8).

We work for justice. We return to prayer. We proclaim what we hear. We are never the same. We are contemplatives on a journey into the heart of our world strengthened by a God who is always One-Who-Is-With-Us.

Your brother,
Don

"We ought acknowledge the particular value of devotion to Mary." (p. 52).
Dominic and Our Lady,
Artist, Henri Matisse, The Rosary Chapel, Vence, France.

8, Preaching in Solidarity with the God of Jesus Christ*

I would like to begin with a sense of mission and our self-identity as Preachers — men and women whose spirituality is formed by the mission of the Word, the Word as the self-communication of God, the Word as enfleshed in history, the Word as proclaimed by preachers, educators, and pastoral ministers. We begin as Preachers not only with the sense of a mission but also with an ecclesial sense and a social sense, and at the same time we perceive the brokenness of both the church and the world in which we presently find ourselves.

As Preachers we know that our mission is the proclamation of the gospel, the good news of the power and compassion of God, the gospel of our Lord Jesus Christ whose death and resurrection give testimony to complex, victimizing, socio-economic, political, and religious forces within which God remains the final judge.

As Preachers, we proclaim the gospel of Jesus Christ not only in a divided world, but in a divided church as well. Indeed, since the Second Vatican Council, and most probably for the next twenty years at least, two conflicting ecclesiologies compete, at times unhealthily, for our absolute allegiance. The eventual authoritative interpretation of Vatican II remains a task for history to determine. But among us our allegiances divide over a vision of church in which hierarchical language is primary and a vision of church for which our institutional structures are essential but secondary, a church more clerically focused for which a theology of ordained ministry becomes paramount and a church perceived as a people grounded in the birthright of their baptism, a church which teaches the world out of the legacy of an authoritative tradition and a church which is a co-learner with the world as well as with non-Christians and non-Catholics as together we read the signs of our history. Many see areas of complementarity between these two contrasting ecclesiologies. Others feel a moral imperative to take sides. The Spirit can indeed work both from above and from below, but each of us gets caught up in the Spirit in our own ways with our own fears, hopes, vulnerabilities, intellectual habits, temperaments, selfishness, and often one-dimensional perspectives.

*. Excerpt from an address on the occasion of the Provincial Assembly, Province of St. Albert the Great, May 26, 1987.

Yet, in the midst of it all, we must begin by calling to mind who we are and why we have been called, that we are all on a mission in this world, all missionaries of the Word, Preachers of the gospel of God.

PREACHING TRUTH

And more than ever we must also call to mind that our deepest commitment as Preachers is to *the truth*. We can talk about truth in many ways, such as objective truth, personal truth, and symbolic truth. We can seek the truth, speak the truth, and do the truth. But what is most obvious is that we live in a world that has lost its love of truth. For it we conveniently substitute personal opinions, misinformation, national security needs, upward socio-economic mobility, and clichés, whether they be contemporary or traditional.

Dominic founded an order of men and women as dedicated to truth as it is to preaching. For his preaching mission to take hold and have importance at his period of history, learning was required, a learning that comes from the Scriptures, from the church, from experience, from prayer, from wisdom, and from an understanding of the times. Indeed Dominic and Francis understood their period of history, read the signs of their times, and saw the need for a new emphasis and movement in religious life. Dominic's grace-filled response to the cues of his world was a family of preachers wholeheartedly dedicated to truth. Thomas' love of truth led him to reading, understanding, and interpreting the secular philosophy of Aristotle and putting it at the service of the gospel. He neither accepted Aristotle uncritically nor rejected him out of hand. As Thomas was formed by Scripture, the fathers of the church, and conciliar teaching, so he could put Aristotle at the service of the tradition he loved and inherited. An act of courage and a miracle when one stops to think of it. Catherine's love of truth led her both to the contemplative experience of the divine mystery, and also to a course of action which had social and political implications as well. Again, when one thinks of this fourteenth-century woman, one cannot help but marvel at her courage in doing the truth. Orthopraxis as well as orthodoxy made her both saint and doctor.

Henri Lacordaire, to whom we owe so much in terms of the benefits we continue to reap from the French Dominicans in our own day, read the signs of the times of his century and pursued a path dedicated to truth, accepting post-revolution France and its liberal ideals, which did not make him popular in the church. But he was also critical of post-revolution France's enlightened intolerance of religion which did not make him popular in the newborn social order. His constant theme was always both *présence au Dieu* and *présence au monde*. His spirit inspired men like Lagrange, Lebret, Chenu, Congar — whose love of truth put all of them on the frontiers of biblical, economic, historical, and ecumenical research. Our mission has always been a mission on the frontiers. Truth took our brother, Bartolomé de las Casas, to the frontiers of a new world in the sixteenth century where his love of justice manifested his radical understanding of the implications of a life turned over to truth.

It is our love of truth that sets us free, gives us courage, and points us in a direction from which we cannot turn. We are Preachers for whom Pilate's question, "What is truth?" is not just a job but a vocation.

IN SOLIDARITY WITH GOD

Our pursuit of truth is equalled by our pursuit of holiness. "Holiness language" and the striving after Christian perfection are no longer popular topics among us. Yet if we return to our roots in Jesus Christ, or to the origins of religious life, or to the life of our father Dominic, or to the inspiration that brought us to a novitiate that would socialize us into a new way of life, we cannot avoid asking the question: does the world perceive us today as holy? And even more so, what does holiness mean in our world today?

Jesus Christ's foundational religious experience was that of an intimacy and solidarity with God which led him to address God almost blasphemously as *Abba*. Antony's, Pachomius', or Benedict's search were simply expressions of their desire to know God. Likewise, to understand Dominic, one must understand his love of the God of Jesus Christ. And so it is for ourselves. Our love of God and thirst for holiness is not something that can take second place. We are here because we seek or at some time sought to know God and to know God more personally.

"Henri Lacordaire read the signs of the times of his century." (p. 56)

Artist,
PLACID STUCKENSCHNEIDER, OP

It would be worthwhile to contrast the heroic and inspirational figure that lies behind the great Greek epic, Ulysses, with the figure that is foundational and patriarchal for the Hebrew Bible, Abraham.[1] The story of Ulysses is the drama of one who longs to return home. The story of Abraham and Sarah is of a couple who leave home and face the unknown. The kind of security that home implies will never be theirs. They live only by faith in themselves and a trust in God's promises. It is the figure of Abraham more than of Ulysses who typifies our own journey.

The question we face then is not whether to be holy, but how to be holy — how to be holy in this latter part of the twentieth-century world. There is no one everlasting definition of what holiness requires.

For Dominic, holiness did not imply being another Benedict. And Dominic's brand of holiness was a scandal for many who had become accustomed to the traditional forms of religious life. Yet Dominic's love and experience of God as well as his capacity to read the signs of his period of history led to a new definition of holiness which affected the history of the world. The same was true of Jesus. The new movement for renewal which he inaugurated within Judaism was based on a new understanding of holiness that was distinctive from the quest for holiness as outlined by Sadducees, Pharisees, or Essenes. Jesus' definition of holiness was that of an inclusive compassion rooted in his own experience of the Father's unlimited love for all.

The form or shape that the striving after holiness will take in our period of history will not be the same as that of first-century Christians or thirteenth-century Christians. Yet we are all defined by that desire to know God more intimately and proclaim God more adequately.

One thing is certain, however. Just as the search for truth cannot be separated from the search for God, no matter what our period of history, so our search for God cannot be separated from our thirst for justice on earth. Because we desire to be holy, we also desire to be just. As the psalmist says, "Holiness and justice support your throne, O God." Indeed, holiness is orthopraxis, not an orthodoxy by itself alone.

PREACHING TRUTH AND JUSTICE

The effort to articulate a renewed understanding of holiness and spirituality lies underneath Edward Schillebeeckx's hermeneutical project.[2] In

1. See John W. Padberg, S.J., "The Past as Prologue", in *Religious Life at the Crossroads*, ed. David Fleming, SM (New York: Paulist Press, 1985), 19.

2. See in particular his *Christ*, (New York: Seabury Press, 1980), 670-743, 762-821, and the collection entitled *God Among Us, The Gospel Proclaimed*, (New York: Crossroad, 1983), 33-44, 85-90, 103-15, 122-27, 164-74, 180-87, 232-48.

Schillebeeckx's spirituality, one's experience of God for Christians leads them into a following after Jesus and "the praxis of the reign of God." Indeed, holiness *is* orthopraxis, not an orthodoxy by itself alone.

Orthopraxis implies an essential relationship between theory and practice. We cannot have one without the other. A major issue facing the church as we enter the twenty-first century is not the relationship between the past (Scripture and tradition) and the present, but is rather that of the relationship between theory and practice, doctrine and life. How the theory manifests itself in the praxis is a critical test of the theory. Jesus' refusal to sanction an orthodoxy separated from orthopraxis lay underneath his critique of sabbath observance, the Law, and the Temple. Jesus' practice of the reign of God, his praxis of God, the praxis to which God calls us cannot be contained by the Law. Hence the Law, while valid, is also relativized by God.

When it comes then to a question of what it means to follow after Jesus, we are confronted by two contrasting experiences, our experience of God and our experience of the history of human suffering, what Schillebeeckx calls the contrast experience. What are we to make of this contrast between the barbarous excess of human misery and a God who wills good? This painful but hope-filled experience of the contrast is the basis of the prophetic awareness that injustice does not have the right to exist.

Christianity does not attempt to explain this history of suffering. Rather followers of Jesus tell a story, the story of the life, suffering, death, and resurrection of Jesus. Given the awareness of the history of human suffering, those who follow after Jesus necessarily involve themselves in that story and in the struggle for justice on earth. Thus Christian love and holiness are necessarily but not exclusively political. "Political love," to use Schillebeeckx's expression, is an urgent form of contemporary holiness.

In Christian holiness there is both a political or social dimension and a mystical or contemplative dimension. Neither the mystical life nor the political life can be discounted. Both Christian mysticism and Christian politics have the same source: the experience of contrast between a God who loves all humanity and the history of human suffering. For the follower of Jesus, the spiritual life cannot be reduced to "personal holiness" alone, nor can social and political life be reduced to their social and political components alone. For Schillebeeckx, "mysticism" is an intense form of the experience of God. "Politics" is an intense form of social engagement, not restricted to professional politicians. Politics without prayer or mysticism becomes barbaric; mysticism without political love becomes sentimental interiority. A Christian involvement in the world is a *religious* praxis, rooted in a particular interpretation of the world, drawing upon the *experience* of the holy.

Moses, a political leader who brought his people liberation, was a mystic "who spoke to God face to face." For Jesus, the mystical experience of God as Abba was the heart and soul of his mission on behalf of the poor. True mysticism has its own intrinsic value, and not just in reference to its social or political consequences, although true mysticism always does have such consequences. "Bourgeois" religion attempts to separate religion and politics, salvation and liberation, whereas authentic Christian salvation implies both.

Christian life and spirituality are intimately tied up with one's concept of salvation, and the meaning of salvation has been one of Schillebeeckx's enduring concerns. "Salvation means being whole"[3] and salvation becomes less than whole if one emphasizes only one dimension of the human — whether this be the socio-political, the personal, or the eschatological. Social liberation is an integral ingredient of the eschatological salvation offered by God. "Personal salvation" is only partial. And likewise for socio-political liberation. If it claims to be total it becomes a new form of servitude, totalitarianism. Human liberation and Christian redemption are not alternatives but are both constitutive elements of Christian hope.

Schillebeeckx has acknowledged his indebtedness to modern Dominicans, particularly Marie-Dominic Chenu, who probably more than anyone else was Schillebeeckx's inspiration. Chenu guided Schillebeeckx's early doctoral dissertation on the sacraments, and it was Chenu who gave substance to the phrase, "signs of the times," in modern Catholic theology.[4] If one wanted to trace the development of modern Catholic thought and spirituality from Chenu through the present writings of Schillebeeckx, one might entitle it, "From the 'Signs of the Times' to 'Political Holiness.'"

Underlying this development, and a key to understanding Schillebeeckx, is the foundational idea of *présence au monde*. The term originated with Lacordaire, was developed by Chenu, had its influence at the Second Vatican Council, and has been consciously acknowledged by Schillebeeckx as influential on his own hermeneutical project. *Présence au monde* is the grace of understanding deeply one's own time and the capacity to respond accordingly.

The two-fold *présence au Dieu* and *présence au monde*, as Lacordaire

3. *Christ*, 717.
4. "Les signes des temps," *La Nouvelle Revue Théologique* (Jan., 1965), 29-39.

had put it, is the same spirit which goes back to Dominic himself who instructed his own followers to speak only to God and about God. The spiritual life is always a parable of God interacting as grace with God's people.

Spirituality is a particular way of being human. It cannot be imposed from the outside or enforced. Yet Christian spirituality never means living "only for God," while others or our history are given second place. Following Jesus can never be a mere repetition of some earlier form of Christian spirituality, but is rather Christian creativity in a historical context. Spirituality is always a new adventure, with Abraham and Sarah as models: "They set out on a journey, not knowing where they were going" (Heb 11:8).

We ought some time not only take the time to study critically the signs of our times but also re-read our own US. history. We assume we know our story, having read it in grade school and again in high school. Yet, as an adult, I have received a different picture, say of Christopher Columbus, than my earlier textbooks had taught, Columbus who had been so warmly greeted by the Arawak Indians when his crew first landed on the Bahamas in 1492, and who by 1495 was sending them back to Spain as slaves from his base on Haiti in the name of the Holy Trinity. Within two years, half of the 250,000 Indians on Haiti were dead from murder, mutilation, or suicide. By 1515, there were perhaps 50,000 Indians left; by 1550, five hundred.[5]

Our chief source of information about what happened on the islands after Columbus came is Bartolomé de las Casas, who transcribed Columbus' journal and wrote a multi-volume *History of the Indies*. Las Casas tells us that the Spaniards "thought nothing of knifing Indians by tens and twenties and of cutting slices off them to test the sharpness of their blades."[6]

Now we may not identify with the atrocities of our forebears and even excuse ourselves from responsibility. We may even excuse ourselves from any responsibility for the black slave trade that made US slavery the most cruel form in all history. And we can excuse ourselves our expansion against Mexico in the name of manifest destiny, our denial of women civil rights, and that we were the first nation to use atomic weapons. We may excuse ourselves of responsibility for all of these.

But we cannot excuse ourselves of present United States policies with

5. See Howard Zinn, *A People's History of the United States* (New York: Harper and Row, 1980), 1-22.

6. Ibid., 6. From Las Casas, *History of the Indies*, Book Two (New York: Harper and Row, 1971).

respect to the arms race, the US-sponsored war in Nicaragua, the US-supported torture and terrorism in other countries. We cannot as a human people, to say nothing of our Christian principles and Catholic tradition, ignore the cry of the poor, the tortured, the unborn, the blacks, women, victims of AIDS, and many others. For these, our history will hold us responsible and on these the God of truth will make a judgment. There simply is no holiness without compassion and no compassion without the capacity for anger at gross injustice and no recourse for gross injustice except social, political, and economic change. Holiness is both deeply mystical and profoundly political. Holiness is based on a life of virtue: of faith, of hope, of a love of enemy, our good sense, thirst for justice, courage and balance. The question facing us today is no longer whether outside the church there is salvation, but rather whether outside of justice, evangelization, and spirituality there is church!

These then are the Preachers that we are called upon to be — proclaiming truth and justice as brothers and sisters. Underlying our message is the centrality of our brotherhood, of our lives together, of our common bonds, of our collaboration with our sisters, of our continuing formation and re-education, our lives of prayer and study.

CONCLUSION

In conclusion, I would like to return to the question I have raised on many occasions: what does it mean for us to be brothers to each other? It is our brotherhood that we share in common, our brotherhood that makes our life and ministry distinctive, our brotherhood that binds us together more deeply than the things that pull us apart.

We do not share the same approaches to theology, the same vision of the church, the same social philosophies, the same talents, the same apostolic interests, the same personality profiles, or the same hopes for the future of the Order.

But we are brothers nevertheless, Dominicans, Preachers, seekers after truth and justice — friars, begging our way through the world in order to proclaim the gospel of Jesus Christ, as we in our own ways have come to experience it and understand it.

How I have come to experience, interpret, and understand the paschal mystery of the life, death, and resurrection of Jesus Christ may be different from your understanding. What I have been called and empowered to do may be different from your call. But it is still Jesus who holds us together — for some unfathomable reason.

Whatever else we may say about others in this room, we can say that they are men of faith, men of hope, men with a deep capacity for love and pain and joy, vulnerable men, weak men, proud men, selfish men, chosen men, broken men, and men of perseverance.

What does it mean to be brothers? It means you are the ones God has given me to love. You are the ones in the midst of whom my own journey toward salvation will take place. You are the ones whom I most hurt and disappoint and the ones who most hurt and disappoint me.

I have seen the grace of brotherhood manifest itself many times during these past two years:

in the way a brother and his community faced death,

in the way our brothers welcome our mothers and fathers and also grieve with us on their loss,

in our continuing to serve the Province in spite of repeated misunderstandings,

in the way so many of you have accepted challenges to confront some particular aspect of your lives and the way others were there when you needed them,

in the way a brother comes to a decision whether to remain among us,

in the trust of a brother who confides in another that he is gay,

in the pain some of you have experienced when feeling the need to say no to me to a particular request,

in the way we express concern and care for our sick,

in our solidarity with our Dominican sisters and laity,

in your willingness to de-emphasize my limitations and accept so well what I have to offer,

in our prayer for each other, and in our love for each other.

Let no one say that brotherhood does not exist among us. To find brotherhood we simply need *to be* brothers. Lord, who is my brother? We become brothers when we share tears, frustrations, aspirations, and celebrations.

Do we have sufficient reason to be hopeful about our future? Yes, if we believe in each other, in the power of prayer, and in the Holy Spirit, the Lord and the Giver of Life.

With Paul the preacher, and in union with Friar Dominic, I can say:

I thank my God whenever I think of you; and every time I pray for all of you, I pray with joy, remembering how you have helped to spread the Good News from the day you first heard it right up to the present. I am quite certain that the One who began this good work in you will see that it is finished when the Day of Christ Jesus comes. It is only natural that I should feel like this toward you all, since you have shared the privileges which have been mine: both my chains and my work defending and establishing the gospel. You have a permanent place in my heart, and God knows how much I miss you all, loving you as Christ Jesus loves you. My prayer is that your love for each other may increase more and more and never stop improving your knowledge and deepening your perception so that you can always recognize what is best. This will help you to become pure and blameless, and prepare you for the Day of Christ, when you will reach the perfect goodness which Jesus Christ produces in us for the glory and praise of God (Phil 1:3-11).

"Our chief source about what happened on the islands after Columbus came is Bartolomé de las Casas." (p. 61).

Artist, PLACID STUCKENSCHNEIDER, OSB

9, Friendship and Brotherhood[1]

Dear Brothers,

Friendship is a value about which we say too little. Indeed, how does this very personal, preferential, and reciprocal form of love fit into our lives within apostolic communities? How does the kind of fidelity friendship requires toward a particular person fit with the kind of fidelity required of us by vows and religious vocation? And yet how can one talk about Dominican life, emphasizing our values of prayer, study, community, ministry and the vows without mentioning friendship? Our friends may be distinct from our brothers, co-workers, and neighbors — all of whom also play an integral role in our lives as Dominicans and with whom friendship may also develop.

We can emphasize friendship as a human value, as a Christian value, or as a specifically Dominican value. Both Plato and Aristotle felt the need to discuss friendship at some length, as did essayists from Cicero to Montaigne. Within Christianity, the subject was perhaps most pointedly addressed from within monasticism, and thus was not foreign to the history of religious life. And yet today there is still a need being felt for a theology of friendship. Dominican tradition gives witness to significant affective bonds within the brotherhood as well as to bonds of friendship beyond the brotherhood — with both women and men.

Our ambiguity and even ambivalence probably stem from the fact that either experientially or intuitively we suspect that profound friendships are not easily integrated into our lives and thus are potentially destructive of the brotherhood, community, and even celibacy. It is often in the context of a close relationship that we are least able to deny that we are sexual beings. We do not have to say that such integration is easy. Nor need we deny potential risks. In previous letters to the Province I have spoken about the value of contemplation and the subject of justice. Would we say that these are easily integrated into our lives? Is that justification for setting them aside? Avoiding their challenge? Is it not potentially destructive to ignore the good that friendship can bring into our lives? And is there not grave risk involved in denying our human sexuality just as there is in affirming it? Who suggests that conceptualizing Dominican life as a life without risk better fits Dominican history at its best than conceptualizing Dominican life as an adventure together with our brothers and sisters?

1. January 28, 1988, Feast of St. Thomas Aquinas

THE GIFT OF FRIENDSHIP

Friendship is a gift, and it is not a gift given to everyone in religious life, for whatever reason. My own conviction is that God wants to give everyone the gift of friendship, but due to sin in the world it is not a gift from which everyone benefits. No one has many friends. We may have many acquaintances, brothers, sisters, co-workers, or "neighbors" (people to whom we minister). But friends are very few.

I myself consider friendship to be one of the greatest gifts of my life — along with the gift of faith and the gift of my religious vocation. Friendship as much as anything, if not more, makes me a grateful man. Knowing true love cannot help but make one a grateful person. I have received through friendship far more than I have given. I make no pretense that friendship is easy or painless. There is nothing that we can ultimately do to secure or guarantee it. Every relationship is affected by human growth and changes in the other person. More is required of us at times than we think we can bear — to let go, to let be, to let another be free. The process by which a friendship is formed is neither a science nor an art. Each friendship is unique, unknown in advance where it may go, a product of both grace and nature. We may find teachers or models along the way, but the path we trod is ever new. Yet I do know, as uncharted as the way of each particular friendship is, that true friends can enhance our sense of brotherhood, our commitment to community, our love of contemplation, our thirst for justice, our fidelity to our call, and our appreciation of the chaste life. True friends do not distract but rather deepen our desire for each of these.

THE GIFT OF FRATERNITY

I suppose that just as spiritual wisdom, including biblical wisdom, has exalted true friendship, so it has warned against false friends. It is not true friendship, but false friendship as well as false selves and egos that attempt to set friendship over against fraternity and community, or to question one's fidelity to contemplation, mission, obedience, and vocation, or create a general disregard or disrespect for the chaste life. Yet friendship in the end teaches us that life is ambiguous, our self-sufficiency insecure, our motives mixed, and that the path to heaven is through our humanity and not through bypassing it. The Incarnate Word himself did not live his human life apart from the joy and the sorrow of human friends. Any human good becomes distorted if it is made the total good, the be-all and end-all of life. But it is equally distorted to deny a particular human good its rightful Christian value.

As friendship is a grace and a gift, so is the brotherhood we share. Both the concept and the reality of brotherhood is something we ought to discuss together more frequently. First, we ought not define friendship and brotherhood over against each other, as if one is a threat to the other, or superior to the other. Second, we need to discover ways to strengthen even further the bonds of our brotherhood at the same time as we compliment each other for sharing our lives together as well as we do.

Sometimes I think, when I emphasize the importance of friends in our lives as religious, that some think I am emphasizing one value at the expense of another. This is not the case. We ought not define friendship over against brotherhood or vice-versa. We are called both to be friends with friends and brothers to our brothers and sisters. One does not diminish the other. Friendship is a very special bond, and so is brotherhood. Socially or psychologically we may at times exaggerate the kind of intimacy we share with our friends and our culture can down-play the kind of intimacy we share as brothers. Yet we know that our society longs for a greater sense of community. It is not something that we North Americans always know a lot about, but it is something that we as religious should know about.

I recall a story told by Sister Ann Willits. When she was quite young, still pre-school age, a neighborhood friend questioned her about their relationship. Ann said, "Well, we can be friends." But her friend replied, "Can't we be more than friends? Can't we be sisters?" Sisterhood and brotherhood are profound and unique bonds. A friend is a priceless gift; so is a brother. This is why I often ask us to reflect on what it means for us to be brothers. Neither friendship nor brotherhood is superior to the other or more important. We are called to love in both ways, indeed several ways — to have our friends as friends, our brothers and sisters as brothers and sisters, and those in need or those to whom we minister as our neighbors. These loves do not compete with each other.

The brotherhood is truly a great gift, and we must be vigilant in building it up. I felt a genuine sense of brotherhood among us as we gathered together in assembly last May. Perhaps we do not look often enough at the real quality of our brotherhood and compliment ourselves.

At the same time, we do need to challenge ourselves further. We can never take brotherhood for granted. It is something at which we must work. We are sometimes at our best when someone is exposed to us at their most vulnerable. But what is the quality of our daily care for one another? How does television affect the quality of our time together and what would be the experience of fraternity without it? How is our fraternal life affected or created or dissipated by the liquor cabinet? How do we celebrate our holidays together? Have we lost something of great importance that too many find experiences of fraternity more outside than inside the community? Where does our energy go?

Just as I have emphasized before that we are contemplatives, apostolic contemplatives but contemplatives nevertheless, so we are friars-preachers, which means friars as well as preachers. Do we emphasize the apostolic side of our lives at the expense of the fraternal side — and at what cost, and at what cost to the apostolate as well?

We are brothers, and we have a growing sense of ourselves as brothers, and there are many exemplifications of the quality of the brotherhood we share. But our brotherhood is also a gift, not one to be taken for granted, one that can suffer from neglect. Community, friendship, and ministry are not incompatible ways of loving. I thank God for both my friends and for you, my brothers. I have been enriched by both; I feel dedicated to both.

THE GIFT OF CHASTITY

A deep respect for friendship and for the brotherhood can enhance our appreciation of chastity — for chastity expresses our respect for both. As a profound commitment to the contemplative life can enable us to see value in obedience and to understand it in a balanced way, so a commitment to friends as friends and our brothers as our brothers can enable us to desire chastity for other than moralistic reasons. When we speak about chastity or about sexuality in our lives, we can easily err in one of two directions —overestimating its importance, or underestimating it.

We have at times done the virtue or vow of chastity a disservice by stressing its importance beyond that of any other virtue or the other vows. It became the sign of supernatural life, the "Catholic" virtue, and sins against chastity the primary confessional matter. On the other hand, it is common today to dismiss chastity altogether, to consider it dated in the modern world, or to think of knowing ourselves sexually as the hallmark of human maturity.

In calling our attention to chastity as befitting our lives as apostles and contemplatives, I do not want to exaggerate its place in our lives out of proportion to its value. Neither do I want to relegate it to the level of the non-discussable or non-important. Nor do I want to assume that we have a common understanding of its implications — any more than there is among us such a completely agreed upon understanding for the implications of the vows of poverty or obedience. What I want to do is simply speak about chastity personally as a value and to emphasize a few points.

Friends have been one of the stronger motivations for my striving to be chaste. Rather than thinking of intimate, particular, reciprocal and committed love as a danger to chastity, I have found the opposite to be true. Being chaste is a way of being true to my friend, a way of being faithful to my friend, a way of loving my friend, whereas casual sexual/genital involvements or a commitment to a genitally sexual relationship will only destroy friendship within religious life or make it impossible. I realize that statements like this require further discussion, but I am only attempting to say that close friendships need not threaten chastity. True friends desire to be chaste and friendship motivates one to live chastely.

Also, the more we identify out lives together as "brothers dwelling together in harmony," the more we will see unchastity as a betrayal of the brotherhood. I am not speaking here about our human sexual struggles and weaknesses which we all have, but rather of a gross disregard for chastity as a value to be pursued. My brother can never become my lover, and having a lover (woman or man) is not fair to my brothers. My most personal motivation for chastity comes from a sense of fidelity and generosity to my brothers and friends. Our vows are not unrelated to the desire to be better friars and preachers.

We approach, as a Province, the feast of our brother, Friar Thomas. A wonderful way to celebrate the gift of Thomas to our Order is to celebrate the gifts of friendship, fraternity, and chastity that have been given us.
Your brother,
Don
1. January 28, 1988, Feast of St. Thomas Aquinas

10, Solidarity with the Poor[1]

Dear Brothers,

As we celebrate the feast of St. Catherine, I would like to reflect on our call to live justly by looking at Pope John Paul II's recent encyclical (December 30, 1987), *Sollicitudo Rei Socialis*, commemorating the twentieth anniversary of Paul VI's *Populorum Progressio* (March 26, 1967).

Section I of the encyclical, the introduction, identifies two dimensions of church teaching, typical of the church's social teaching: continuity and newness, a continuity with respect to its fundamental orientation, and renewal given changing historical and social conditions (Par. 3).

Section II is a reflection on Paul VI's encyclical, *Populorum Progressio*, particularly its originality as seen from within the context of the church's continuous social concern. John Paul II sees his own social teaching as in continuity with that of Paul VI and also a further development of Paul VI's analysis. John Paul recognizes the duty of the church "to scrutinize the signs of the times," as we have been directed to do by Vatican II in *Gaudium et Spes*. He summarizes the originality of *Populorum Progressio* in three points:

1. Paul VI emphasized the ethical or moral character of problems connected with the human development of peoples, problems which at first sight seem to be solely social or economic in nature. Thus given the moral character of these issues, the church cannot be accused of going beyond her sphere of competence in addressing them. The church has the right and obligation to address the social questions of our day because they are also ethical questions (Par. 8).

2. The "social question" has assumed global, international, worldwide proportions, which does not diminish the importance of national or local concerns but does place these latter issues in a wider context. "Therefore political leaders and citizens of rich countries, considered as individuals, especially if they are Christians, have the moral obligation ... to take into consideration in personal decisions and decisions of government ... this interdependence which exists between their conduct and the poverty and underdevelopment of so many millions of people" (Par. 9).

3. Paul VI provided an original contribution to the church's own understanding when he wrote, "Development is the new name for peace," (*Populorum Progressio*, 87). The demand for justice can only be satisfied

1. April 29, 1988, Feast of St. Catherine of Siena

within a global context, but it must also be said that "war and military preparations are the major enemy of the integral development of peoples" (John Paul II, Par. 10).

The above observations only re-enforce the teaching of the United States Bishops in their pastorals on peace and on the economy, the interdependence of these two issues, their global repercussions, and their moral character.

Sections III and IV of the encyclical are John Paul II's social analysis of our situation twenty years later. It provides the basis for the ways in which he goes beyond what Paul VI was able to address.

From an economic point of view, the situation in the world has noticeably worsened. The Pope utilizes language about the gap between the North and the South, which has widened, as well as language which speaks of the First World, Second World, Third World, and even Fourth World (the bands of extreme poverty in countries of medium or high income). The unity of the human race is being compromised, and the church as a "sacrament . . . of the unity of the whole human race" cannot be indifferent (Par. 14).

John Paul then proceeds in his analysis from these economic issues to a political analysis, to a fact which had considerable impact on the development of peoples since World War II, namely, the two opposing blocs, the East and the West, at whose feet he places equal blame and responsibility. "For we know the tension between East and West is not in itself an opposition between two different levels of development but rather between two concepts of the development of individuals and peoples, both concepts being imperfect and in need of radical correction . . . This is one of the reasons why the church's social doctrine adopts a critical attitude toward both liberal capitalism and Marxist collectivism . . ." (Par. 21). I know of no papal statement of the church's social teaching that specifies Western capitalism so clearly as a source of social irresponsibility among nations.

After a focus on John Paul's socio-economic concerns, and then geopolitical concerns, he turns his attention to ecological concerns as well. With reference to a civilization of "consumption" or "consumerism," and "the injustice of the poor distribution of the goods and services originally intended for all" (Par. 29), John Paul teaches that "the dominion granted to man by the Creator is not an absolute power nor can one speak of a freedom to 'use and misuse' or to dispose of things as one pleases" (Par. 34).

Section V moves to a moral-theological analysis of the economic, political, and ecological issues addressed. Here John Paul clearly calls upon the contemporary theological emphasis on "structures of sin" (Par. 36) as well as the "virtue of solidarity"(Par. 38, 40). He develops an understanding of the virtue of solidarity: the solidarity of the poor among themselves, the awareness of interdependence as needing to be transformed into a solidarity based upon the principle that the goods of creation are meant for all, and solidarity as the path to peace and development (Par. 38, 39). By maintaining continuity with the concerns of *Populorum Progressio*, and by a social analysis of the world twenty years later, John Paul II renews Catholic social teaching by his contribution of a theology of solidarity as a Christian virtue.

From an emphasis on solidarity in Section V of the encyclical, he goes on in Section VI to emphasize the direction that the church's social teaching is taking.

Today more than in the past, the church's social doctrine must be open to an international outlook, in line with the Second Vatican Council, the most recent encyclicals and particularly in line with the encyclical which we are commemorating. It will not be superfluous therefore to re-examine and further clarify in this light the characteristic themes and guidelines dealt with by the magisterium in recent years.

Here I would like to indicate one of them: the option or love of preference for the poor. This is an option or a special form of primacy in the exercise of Christian charity to which the whole tradition of the church bears witness. It affects the life of each Christian inasmuch as he or she seeks to imitate the life of Christ, but it applies equally to our social responsibilities and hence to our manner of living, and to the logical decisions to be made concerning the ownership and use of goods.

Today, furthermore, given the worldwide dimension which the social question has assumed, this love of preference for the poor, and the decisions which it inspires in us, cannot but embrace the immense multitudes of the hungry, the needy, the homeless, those without medical care and, above all, those without hope for a better future. It is impossible not to take account of the existence of these realities. To ignore them would mean becoming like the "rich man" who pretended not to know the beggar Lazarus lying at his gate (cf. Luke 16:19-31) (Par. 42).

In concluding, John Paul points to strengths and limitations in liberation theology, to the knowledge that no temporal achievement can be identified with the kingdom of God, and to the process of authentic development and liberation as taking concrete shape "in the exercise of

'Names like St Martin de Porres.... come immediately to mind' in the context of the priority of the call of the poor. (p. 42).

Artist, ALBERT CARPENTIER, OP

solidarity, that is to say, in the love and service of neighbor, especially of the poorest" (Par. 46).

I can think of no better way to celebrate the feast of St. Catherine than to call to mind her own love for the sick and the poor, to reflect further on the challenge to which this solidarity with the poor calls us, and to read prayerfully and thoughtfully John Paul II's encyclical and to connect it with what next steps we need to take.

May the God of the poor continue both to embrace and to challenge us.

Yours in Dominic and Catherine,
Don

11, Community Life[1]

Dear Brothers,

We are once again celebrating the feast of Albert the Great. As we do so, let us think about community life. What are the major obstacles to community life? What is the most important issue communities face as we attempt to strengthen life together? What should be emphasized as most important for us? Here are some possible considerations.

OBSTACLES TO COMMUNITY LIFE

1. *Self-rejection.* A healthy community requires healthy people, and there is nothing more important to mental health than self-acceptance and self-confidence. A community cannot give me these and a community is not to blame if I lack them. There are many facets of life that contribute to self-esteem or lack thereof: my attitudes about my body, early parental messages and my relationship to both mother and father, a sense of professional competence, the capacity for adult relationships with both men and women, accepting disowned portions of myself, the inability to perceive and accept the truth about myself. In order to live in community, I must first of all be able to live with myself. Self-rejection leads to destructive attitudes and projections.

2. *Jealous Competition.* All of us experience jealousy in varied ways. Few human beings are immune to it. It can be even more forceful when living together. The challenge is what to do with these deeply felt rivalries. Jealousy is rooted in the competitive spirit and in comparative thinking. If we have a secure self-image (number one above), we will not need to find security and re-assurance by comparing ourselves to others. We will only compare ourselves anyway on those points or to those people wherein we are most vulnerable. We can diminish the hold jealousy has on us by refusing to make comparisons. We can then begin to appreciate and affirm the talents and gifts of each brother and our self-worth will not depend upon putting others down. Growing up male in the United States means learning to achieve, to make comparisons, and to be competitive — whether in athletics, academics, work or relationships. As religious men, we must seek our sense of worth apart from rivalries and competition for attention. Being the center of attention on a regular basis is incompatible with community life. Habits of jealousy lead to scapegoating — an all too frequent occurence.

3. *Passive Aggression.* Most of us have been socialized into thinking

1. November 15, 1988, Feast of St. Albert the Great

of anger as bad. Anger as willing harm on someone is morally wrong. But anger as an emotion is morally neutral — it depends upon what I do with the anger, how I express it. There is probably more repressed anger among religious than any other emotion. We must learn how to express anger constructively. We can't allow it to harden, like resentment, into cement. One of the common ways among religious of coping destructively with anger is through passive or indirect hostility, or even converting the anger into an untouchable "niceness." Much passive aggression can be found in addictive and co-dependent systems and organizations. We have all probably experienced passive aggression. We must check ourselves for its presence within us as well. It can kill community life. Typical passive aggressive behaviors include obstructionism, procrastination, stubbornness, chronic complaining, backbiting, intentional inefficiency, surface niceness, and the refusal to speak directly to someone. We all get angry. There is nothing wrong with that. But we can all ask ourselves what we then do with that anger.

ISSUES OF IMPORTANCE IN COMMON LIFE

1. *The Reality and the Ideal.* Community life requires a developed sense of balance. The newer or younger members of the Province are often attracted by the ideal of common life. Yet they slowly learn to balance that ideal with the realities they experience as they come to know us better. On the other hand, those of us who are older in the Province have too often given up, or given in to the attitude that this is all there is. We need to balance a complacency or cynicism with the ideal to which we are called. It is easier to live an extreme, either as a romantic or as a cynic. But Christian life and religious life are neither. There is more to common life than the ideal alone: there are people, like us, imperfect and vulnerable and human and not always likeable. Community life is about people, not an idea. I recall an old Peanuts cartoon: "Humanity I love: it's people I can't stand." Community life is learning to live together as brothers — with its pains and its joys. At the same time, community does not have to mean living the lowest common denominator. The common life is a call, a challenge, an invitation, a form of discipleship, something which calls us to a deeper life. We constantly need to check our sense of balance. Do I expect too much? Have I given up? Do the others have to meet my expectations? Have I gotten into a "rut"? Can I be more accepting and understanding? Is it time someone calls my bluff and calls me back to live what I say I believe? Whose conscience am I examining now?

2. *Intimacy and Community.* These two elements in our lives also reflect the need for balance. Last January, for the feast of Saint Thomas,

I wrote about friendship and fraternity, but they deserve to be mentioned again in this context. We all have the need for human intimacy, for relationships that involve more personal disclosure and sharing. Yet we can never define community in terms of those needs. Community and intimacy are not the same. We are communities of brothers, not friends. We cannot expect that a particular local community will meet all our needs for intimacy. We need to be able to balance friendship and brotherhood, just as we do ministry, community, and prayer. To say that our communities are not based on living with friends does not imply that we do not have friends among the Province members. If all our friends were outside the Province, it would diminish our provincial life. Yet we cannot expect that every brother be a friend. Nor should we disparage the profound character of being brothers. Brotherhood is not inferior to friendship, simply another form of commitment and love. In any case, our struggles to balance our commitment to the brotherhood and our needs for intimacy raises many other issues for us: areas of sexuality, what being male means, how we relate to each other as men, how we relate to women, our differences in temperament, affective maturity, homophobia, misogynism — all those vulnerable issues that we need to face within ourselves if we are going to relate to others just at a human level.

3. *Community and Commitment.* There can be no such thing as community, particularly religious community, without commitment — not only to the way of life but even more so to each other. As the authors of *Habits of the Heart* pointed out, commitment does not come easy for us. Yet, if life together is going to work, we must be committed to each other and to the Province — and commitment implies investment of ourselves in our mission and in our common life. Commitment involves sacrifice. There is a true sense in which we do leave "the world" behind and all the world offers by way of competition for our attention. This does not mean that religious commitment is world-negating. We leave some things — career options, life styles, independence in decision making, a genital sexual life — for the sake of something else, ultimately for the sake of the gospel. People make up a community, and only community members make the community work. Commitment is not only a question of whether people are able to make lasting commitments these days, but even more so whether those finally professed for several or many years are able to sustain at more than a superficial level the commitment they made. What do I sacrifice for others in community? What is the level of my investment? To what degree am I trying to make community work? Which comes first — my interests or the community? Do I have more friends outside or inside the community? Where do I spend my holidays?

All these questions reflect one's level of commitment.

NECESSITIES FOR COMMUNITY

1. *Forgiveness.* There are some "skills" that are almost prerequisites if we are to live together as brothers. First is a constant openness to forgiving others. This is such a central element in gospel life that one would think it hardly needs to be mentioned. How many times in our life have we prayed, "Father, forgive us our trespasses as we forgive those who trespass against us"? How often have we preached on reconciliation? How often have we emphasized the distinctiveness of love of enemy in the teaching of Jesus? Yet we discover that forgiveness is no simple task — easier to recommend than to do. Forgiveness is not a denial of feelings, hurt, pain, anger — and then experiencing them in a more passive and destructive way. Forgiveness is a willingness to let go of grievances, not to harbor resentment, and not to dismiss or cut another out of my life. We may need periods of self-protection when we are most vulnerable, but we need in time to be sure that we remain open to the other. I have found too many members in the Province who are still living out of old or former hurts. Community requires a capacity to forgive.

2. *Humor.* We all ought stop for a moment and make a confession: I take myself too seriously! The importance I attach to my concerns, my opinions, my problems, loses perspective. Few things in life are truly important. If only we could view our problems from the perspectives of those struggling with death, hunger, or hopelessness. If only we could see the cross from the perspective of the resurrection. If only our present concerns could be placed in the context of God's eternity. We take far too many things with a kind of ultimate seriousness. We need to be able to laugh, to laugh at ourselves, to have a sense of humor, a sense of perspective. Being brothers means being able to disagree, to fight, but also to laugh, to celebrate, to have fun — together as brothers. There is no substitute for a sense of humor. Playing together is a part of living together.

3. *Prayer.* The foundation of community life is prayer — intense, personal, communal, and liturgical. Perhaps in the past we have been too facile in recommending prayer as a kind of cure-all for any problem when some problems require other kinds of attention. But today we are perhaps too facile in recommending psychological counseling as a kind of cure-all when it may be our spiritual lives that need to be shaken. We often relegate attention to the spiritual life to the period of initial formation, after which we set about the tasks of ministry. Nothing could be more

detrimental to us personally, to our ministries, and to community life. I am not thinking of anything extraordinary here. But I am thinking of perseverance in the life of prayer. Yves Congar once said, "I am not sure if I have been given the grace of prayer, but I have been given the grace of fidelity to prayer." If there were one single wish which I could be granted on behalf of the Province, it would be that prayer take hold of each of us even more deeply.

These are only some possible responses to the earlier questions I raised. There are others which will come from your own reflection. We cannot allow ourselves to diminish the value of community life. Although never easy, and at times more of an asceticism, it usually rewards us in proportion to the investment we make in it. If we have little positive we can say, we should begin by looking at ourselves first. What has gone wrong? How can I begin to remedy that? To whom can I turn to help me?

Community life is one way we preach the gospel. Community life makes our preaching and our vocation credible. Community gives testimony to what we say we believe. Life in community gives the members their authority.

Your brother,
Don

"The foundation of community life is prayer,
intense, personal, communal and liturgical."

Artist, ALBERT CARPENTIER, OP

12, The Laity[1]

Dear Brothers,

Ecclesiology lies at the heart of many issues we face. No other area of theology today has such far-reaching implications. When it comes to our understanding and vision of church, we in the church and in the province are not of one mind. This is a sign that we must think even more deeply and remain in conversation with those whose theology of the church is a contrast to our own. Central to any theology of the church is that of a theology of the laity.

Our brother, Yves Congar, gave his entire life to ecclesiology, ecumenism, and the theology of the laity. He once said that the most important decision of the Second Vatican Council was the decision to reverse the order of the second and third chapters of the Constitution on the Church *(Lumen Gentium)*. In the earlier draft, the chapter on the church as hierarchical was followed by a chapter on the church as the people, the people of God, and it was decided to reverse the order of these two chapters, giving first place and prominence to the image of the church as God's people. This decision put the laity at the center of post-conciliar awareness.

In 1979 M D Chenu reflected on the social teaching of the church in a short book. For him, the Copernican revolution in theology, especially in the area of social teaching, has been a move toward a more inductive approach — a listening church as well as a teaching church. Again, the laity, their own experience, and the ministry of all the baptized is brought into the foreground. A more inductive approach to moral teaching implies that we are all co-learners even though we may have different responsibilities.

The relationship of the church to the world *(Gaudium et Spes)* and a proper understanding of laity *(Lumen Gentium)* are two of the significant ecclesial issues which face us — and for which none of us has all the answers. The church, both as mystery and as institution, requires an openness on all our parts to continuing reflection. The church, as the communion of the faithful, requires that we continue to think about the faithful, the *sensus fidelium*, and the laity.

THE LAITY AND THE CHURCH

In a laity-centered church, there is an increasing emphasis on the theology

1. January 28, 1989, Feast of St. Thomas Aquinas

of baptism, on the awareness that every baptized Christian has a vocation, on the common vocation to discipleship, on discipleship as manifest in a variety of ministries in the life of the church, and on the interconnectedness of vocation, mission, ministry, and spirituality. These latter are not primarily the prerogative of priests and religious and only secondarily applied to the laity. A church focused on the laity is not primarily clerical. It rather emphasizes participative styles of leadership, recognizes the inadequacy of the clergy/laity distinction within ecclesial life, and affirms adult Christians and also the rite for the Christian initiation of adults as normative for our self-understanding as God's people.

Already in 1953 Congar had published *Towards a Theology of the Laity*. At that time he was still defining the laity in terms of the clergy. Since then, however, he said, after fifty years of thinking about the church, "that the clergy need to be defined in relation to the laity, who are quite simply members of the people of God animated by the Spirit" (*Fifty Years of Catholic Theology, Conversations with Yves Congar,* Fortress Press, 1988, 65-66).

The decision of the Second Vatican Council to focus attention on the laity, on a church of the laity, on the church as God's people, has left many questions for which there are as yet no answers and about which we cannot be naive. The transition from a "clerical church" to a "lay church" is a "Copernican revolution." No revolution, or paradigm shift, or theological development, whether gradual or dramatic, takes place with ease. Nor is there a blueprint in advance. Hence all the more reason for the various sectors of the church to remain in contact and dialog — as conversation partners — for the sake of the church, for the sake of the gospel. None of us can assume at this point that all the truth is on one side of current debates. Sometimes a commitment to truth necessitates taking sides, and sometimes it necessitates sustaining dialog in the midst of conflict until a better apprehension of the truth emerges.

THE LAITY AND THE DOMINICAN FAMILY

An ecclesiology focused on the laity has implications for our understanding of religious life and the Dominican tradition in particular. We can be deeply appreciative of the contribution that some of our members have made to ecclesiology out of the context of their Dominican experience (e.g., Chenu, Congar, O'Meara). Dominicans in particular have given attention to the theology of lay preaching (Schillebeeckx, Hill, Hilkert). But the Order of Preachers perhaps confronts the emerging theology of the laity most clearly in the language and self-understanding of the Order as the Dominican family.

"The Dominican family" is an expression used in the Dominican Constitutions (Basic Constitution, #9; Chapter V, 141-53), but was given explicit and formal status in the Acts of the General Chapter at Tallaght (1971), "The name Order of Preachers in its universal character is the same as Dominican Family" (#122). Also see the prologues to chapter ten of the Acts of the General Chapter of Madonna dell'Arco, 1974, and chapter six of the Acts of the General Chapter of Quezon City, 1977. The statement from the General Chapter of Quezon City is worth quoting at length:

> The Dominican Order must at all times, both in its life and in its work, be alert to the great authentic movements of the age in which it finds itself. This contemporaneous quality was a special mark of the original vision of St. Dominic in founding the Order, and imparted to it its original force and freshness....
>
> At this time, the Order is confronted with two great movements in the Church and in the world: the emergence of the laity as an indispensable element in the establishing of the Kingdom of God, and the more recent and constantly growing movement toward the liberation of women and the recognition of their equality with men. Indeed, both of these movements are but a fulfillment of the words of St. Paul: "There is neither Jew nor Greek, neither slave nor free, neither male nor female, but all are one in Christ." (Gal, 3:28)....
>
> The branches of the Dominican Family are bound together by a common name and by the common apostolic and spiritual traditions which have their source in St. Dominic....
>
> St. Dominic created his family, not for itself, but to be at the service of the Church and its mission to the world. In terms of human potential there are vast resources within the Family. We must admit that, because of a lack of cooperation, this tremendous potential is not fully realized. The development of an authentic Dominican spirit and of Dominican formation have suffered because of the lack of closer bonds within the Dominican Family. The mutual development of vocations which could have taken place has also suffered. Most seriously, there has been a diminished effectiveness of each branch of the family, due to a lack of mutual enrichment between them, leading to one-dimensional viewpoints. It is the genius of the Order that there is in principle a wonderful balance whereby each of the branches of the family reinforces and supplements the others. But unless this delicate balance is maintained, the total apostolate of the Order suffers....
>
> This is indeed a great moment for the Dominican Order to fulfill

that initial vision of St. Dominic, its founder. The two world-wide movements toward an emerging laity and full equality for women coincide in a singular manner with what St. Dominic has sown within the very idea of the Order. That seed and the season for its harvest have at this moment in history come together.

Now is the acceptable time for the Dominican Family to achieve true equality and complementarity among its different branches. If we believe that the Holy Spirit truly speaks to us in and through the signs of the times, we cannot ignore this call to develop among all the branches of the Order a greater collaboration in all our ministries, and we cannot neglect to undertake efforts to study and promote a greater organic unity between these branches. What lies before us at this time is a challenge to become what St. Dominic had begun: a Family joined in unity of life and complementarity of service to the Church and the World.

Both the Chapter at Quezon City and the following chapter at Walberberg (1980) urged the convening of a world-wide assembly or symposium on the Dominican family, which eventually convened in Bologna in 1983 and produced the Bologna document on the Dominican family. This document affirmed various forms of lay affiliation with the Order, challenged Dominican laity to show its contemporaries "an authentic apostolic lay spirituality," and recognized the varied and complementary ways in which the charism of Dominic can be expressed. The document was significant in asserting at least two ways in which laity are members of the Dominican family and share in the spirituality of the Order, the more traditional Dominican laity affiliated with the Order through the friars and by profession, and newer forms of affiliation with different structures, such as associates affiliated with the congregations of our sisters. In an even broader sense, Dominican laity can include those many who serve us with continuing dedication or who serve in our varied apostolates. "Dominican laity" is no longer a univocal expression. Given the emphasis in ecclesiology today on laity, we should be particularly attentive to the laity affiliated with the Order. The majority of the members of the Dominican family are lay Dominicans. (Accurate world-wide statistics are difficult to obtain, but several years ago there were 4,775 nuns, 7,200 friars, 70,431 laity, 40,816 sisters, and 392 members of secular institutes within the Dominican Family.)

IN CONCLUSION

As ecclesiology recognizes the centrality of laity in the life of the church, we ought not neglect their role in the Order. The laity can particularly help prevent the friars from becoming a "clerical" order in the pejorative sense of that term and make us realize that we too must understand Dominican priesthood in relationship to the vocation to Dominican life and "in relation to the laity." We are first of all Dominicans, Preachers, friars, and ordained ministry must be understood in terms of service to an ecclesially conscious lay church.

Best wishes to all of you for the feast of St. Thomas.

Your brother,
Don

"Already in 1953 Yves Congar had published
Towards a Theology of the Laity."

Artist, PLACID STUCKENSCHNEIDER, OSB

13, Evangelization, Contemplation and Justice[1]

Dear Brothers,

The need for evangelization is surfacing again in the life of the Church. Pope Paul VI wrote, "Evangelization is the essential mission of the church" (Evangelii Nuntiandi, 14). What does this mean for us as the Order of Preachers?

EVANGELIZATION

Evangelization ("gospelization") is proclaiming and spreading the gospel of God in word and deed. It implies that we ourselves understand "the gospel." If we cannot articulate it for ourselves, we cannot proclaim it, do it, or be it.

Evangelization announces a conversion, a call to a new way of life, the challenge to live differently. Often, especially for those who have been raised in a Christian culture, conversion is not a dramatic once-and-for-all reversal of life but takes place in stages.

The following stages come from the reflections of Ralph Rogawski on his own experience in preaching with the poor. They make us aware that evangelization takes time to take hold of people's lives. In a letter Ralph wrote:

1. Things begin to happen by talking, *by announcing the presence of the risen Christ*, either in preaching or in simple conversation. This creates "a moment of grace." I depend upon people's experiencing grace that pertains to their present condition. This is seen more clearly when the people are truly poor.

2. My purpose during the week-long mission is simply to bring people to an adult, personal, free, new, explicit *basing of their lives on Jesus Christ* as the source of graces experienced (like renewal of baptismal promises on Holy Saturday). Their free acceptance in this way has multiple effects which I attribute to the action of the Spirit among them. Although these are personal effects, a small *desire for community* almost always happens, and a new dynamic begins to take shape in their lives.

3. With time, and the experience of this community of faith within a definite socio-political-economic-cultural context, the neighborhood grows. This is a basic element of church which has multiple, observ-

1. January 28, 1990, Feast of St. Thomas Aquinas

able, and surprising effects, which can be called "a new way of living": a new way of thinking, faith as a source of inspiration, a new awareness of dignity, a deeper perception of socio-political reality. Community life becomes the norm. What surprises me is that even though these people are really poor, they don't consider themselves to be as poor as others whom they find to be poorer, and they reach out to minister to others in creative ways. Action is there. It is spontaneous and creative.

4. The next stage is the concern to communicate to their families the values they have received. They sense acutely that social justice is rooted in their family relationships which need to be changed, healed, reconciled, straightened out. This is the area of *the transformation of family life and personal life* which involves: a new sense of personal dignity lived out; a new interest in Scripture as a source of inspiration; a reordering of personal/family attitudes and activities and prioritizing one's use of time; a discovery of charisms (graces) as real, and a reinterpretation of one's life in the light of faith.

5. Next comes the stage of more observable action on behalf of *justice as flowing from the gospel* and their new way of life. The justice concerns are closely related to two areas of life: (a) the location where they live (neighborhood, town, housing project) and its related structures which touch economics, education, culture, local government, associations; and (b) their occupation (or unemployment) and its concomitant concerns which touch labor law, creative jobs, cooperatives, labor unions, political activity, choosing compassionate professions.

Returning to our own situation, the more frequent challenge may be the evangelization of the middle class (including ourselves). The middle class poses a specific challenge since they have assimilated so strongly the American Dream which has become their dominant motivation. Middle class implies people who have taken on the values of the rich. *Conversion implies a move from the values of the rich to the needs of poor.* Conversion implies not only a change of motivation but a change in the direction of one's life. The same stages as above will be analogously applicable (eg, awareness of the presence of the risen Christ, basing one's life on Jesus Christ and a community, a new way of living with action on behalf of justice). Conversion for the middle class (as well as ourselves) also involves a diagnosis or awareness of the particular social situation of the middle class and make us aware of its reality, namely, aimlessness, boredom, and emptiness, masked by consumerism, drugs, and the manufacture of ever-new needs. The middle class too needs to hear the gospel and are of great importance if the social issues of our day are to be addressed.

There are particular obstacles to the evangelization of the middle class of which we need to be aware. Among these are: (1) secularism, and its indifference to religious values; (2) fundamentalism, and its various forms of authoritarianism inside the church and outside; (3) cultural imperialism, or the sense of superiority about one's own culture, and the failure to appreciate and respect those who are marginal by our cultural standards. Perhaps the major obstacle to our own conversion, however, is our neglect of the contemplative life.

CONTEMPLATION

Effective evangelization is rooted in the gospel of God and our very own human experiences of God. As ministers of the Word, we must root ourselves ever more deeply in God. We can never announce God without having first met God. It is God whom we proclaim, the God of Jesus, the God of people, and not ourselves, nor some particular social order. Preaching begins with God, or our experience of God, or our experience of the Spirit, our wilderness experiences — however we express it.

Too often we think that we can get by, fool people, or pretend, by learning something about God, or the Scriptures, or the needs of our world, and this may give us something insightful to say. But we cannot speak about God without having first spoken intensely to God. To attempt to do otherwise is to put cart before horse, to run the risk of confusing the message, or to reveal eventually our spiritual bankruptcy.

We meet God in prayer. This does not mean we encounter God only in solitude. We encounter God in those to whom we minister, those who are in need, among those who are poor or socially marginal, as well as in those who minister to us. The starting point for prayer is our human experiences of God as One-Who-Is-With-Us (Is 7:14).

If our primary mission is that of preaching and evangelization, we must attend to our relationship with God, give ourselves over to prayer, and be with God contemplatively as with a friend. We cannot emphasize our call as Preachers without also emphasizing our vocation as contemplatives.

I have on other occasions emphasized this need to renew the contemplative dimension of our lives. Here I wish to specify three forms that our experiences of God or contemplative prayer can take: the prayer of pain, the prayer of hope, and the prayer of joy.

1. *The Prayer of Pain.* Sometimes our hearts are broken. We allow

ourselves a deeper glimpse of the desperation and loneliness in life. This may come from our empathy with those who struggle to survive, with those who have become victims of hostility, fear, or greed, or it may come from our brothers or sisters or friends or those with whom we work. It may be that something has touched us and opened up wounds we hold within ourselves, or a new awareness that has led us to see or hear or feel that to which we were previously blind or deaf or insensitive. Pain is one form that contemplation can take. Pain at least gives the shape to some of our prayer. It is not a form of prayer to be avoided. To refuse to be with our pain or to pray from within our pain is to close ourselves off to our humanity and run the risk of becoming inhumane.

2. *The Prayer of Hope.* The foundation for the prayer of hope is twofold. It is first of all grounded in an act of faith, namely, "I believe in the Holy Spirit, Lord and giver of Life." The Holy Spirit is both the source of diversity and the cause of unity. Secondly, our hope is proportionate to our capacity to pray with our pain. Pain without hope leads to resentment. Hope without struggle is an illusory and naive optimism. We must ask ourselves in prayer how to sustain hope in the midst of conflicts we experience in our world and our church. The following have been helpful to me: (1) We need a sense of history if we are to be people of hope. (2) We need to deepen our capacity to embrace that which causes us pain or disappointment (a human relationship, our church, our country), as Catherine of Siena embraced the leper (which was also one of her images for church). (3) We need to recognize solidarity in powerlessness (better people than we have been powerless). (4) We need to work for that which we do not expect to see in our own lifetimes. Hope and expectation are not the same.

Rubem Alves makes some of these same points in his*Hijos de Maòana.*

What is hope?
It is a presentiment that imagination is more real
and reality less real than it looks.
It is the hunch
that the overwhelming brutality of facts
that oppress and repress is not the last word.
It is a suspicion
that reality is more complex
than realism wants us to believe
and that the frontiers of the possible
are not determined by the limits of the actual
and that in a miraculous and unexpected way

life is preparing the creative events
which will open the way to freedom and resurrection.
The two, suffering and hope, live from each other.
Suffering without hope
produces resentment and despair,
hope without suffering
creates illusions, naiveté and drunkenness.
Let us plant dates
even though those who plant them will never eat them.
We must live by the love of what we will never see.
This is the secret discipline.

It is a refusal to let the creative act
be dissolved in immediate sense experience
and a stubborn commitment to the future of our grandchildren.
Such disciplined love
is what has given prophets, revolutionaries and saints
the courage to die for the future they envisaged.
They make their own bodies
the seed of their highest hope.
(from *Tomorrow's Children*)

3. *The Prayer of Joy.* One cannot enter into friendship with God without moments of profound gladness, without experiences of grace, without hearts bursting with gratitude. Gratitude may well be the supreme sign of a holy person. To know oneself well and to know God well make for a life of gratitude. True humility and genuine gratitude are two sides of a coin. If a person is grateful, compassion, generosity, and fidelity follow. A sense of gratitude leads to the prayer of joy. We overflow. We praise and bless. We give thanks. Joy is a gift of the Spirit, a sign of the presence of the Spirit. But there can be no true prayer of joy that has bypassed praying with pain and with hope. We must pray in all three ways. Dominican contemplation is the foundation of Dominican preaching. Contemplation provides the roots. Preaching is the tree. The tree then bears a harvest of justice (James 3:18).

JUSTICE

The fruit of contemplation is a bold preaching, evangelization, and catechesis. The fruit of effective preaching will be a thirst for justice. If evangelization is effective, a social consciousness follows. Our path to a more just social order is rooted in the gospel and is the fruit of the gospel. There is no true justice without the gospel. Where the gospel is truly planted, a love for justice will flourish. Justice is the fruit of effective evangelization; effective evangelization grows forth from the contemplative life. The contemplative life is rooted in God. The search for justice does not bypass contemplation and conversion but passes through them. Contemplation and evangelization open the door to justice as an imperative of the gospel and as the evangelical way of life. If we were to do a very unsophisticated analysis of our social situation, especially but not exclusively of the middle class, a significant observation is forthcoming: there is widespread ignorance of justice as a constitutive element of the gospel — the failure to internalize the truth that God wants us to live and act justly.

This observation is not an effort to place blame but rather to understand. Our situation flows from the way that the Catholic faith has been preached and taught. By and large, we taught and were taught a double standard: If you want to follow Jesus radically, you do so in religious life, which implies to some degree leaving the concerns of the world behind. If you are not called to this radical form of discipleship, it is sufficient to follow the church's teaching on personal and family morality and participate in the sacraments. In those areas that pertain to public, economic, and political life, you by and large are forced to follow the way of "the real world." Our way of preaching and teaching created a dichotomy between the personal and the public — and this is what most good Catholics have learned, to live Christian lives at home and not to worry about how being Christian affects the world of business or government. Thus the challenge which confronts us today, partly of our own making, is how to help people put these two halves of their lives together. Neither our theology of religious life nor our theology of the laity have prepared us for what it means to be church in the midst of our world.

Our present reality is partly the effect of a preaching and teaching that were effective. We are up against a Catholicism that some have called "the second collection syndrome": being Christian means being good to your family and friends, being decent in the business world and paying your taxes, and if you have something left over you can give to charities.

We cannot assume that those to whom we preach know what justice as understood in the Bible means. It is not a question of ill will, or even socio-economic status. The gospel has never been preached in a way that enabled people to hear and understand that *God wants justice*. No one has sufficiently explained that the biblical concept of justice is something to which we are obliged. We can look at the fate of the bishops' pastoral on the economy. On the one hand, we fail to preach and teach it. On the other hand, we try to do so, and we often do so ineffectively. We do not sufficiently understand the situation of our hearers who do not know that economic justice is part of Catholic faith and tradition. If we are honest, we have to admit that even as Preachers we are not sure of how to go about the kind of evangelical preaching that leads to the thirst for justice.

Take for example the expression "preferential option for the poor" with all its evocative power. To most Catholics, and certainly to the middle class, does it make sense? What does it mean? Does it not sound unfair? It goes against the grain of what we have conscientiously assimilated as North Americans and as Catholics. Yet can we not understand using the language of a family, the special care or concern that is rightly shown a member who is disabled or disadvantaged in some way? Is such special attention unfair?

A preaching which bears fruit in the conversion of people to justice and the needs of the poor as an imperative of the gospel is grounded in our life of Dominican contemplation and the demands of a commitment to study. Ignorance is not removed by ignorance, but by learning and right thinking.

Preaching justice is rooted in our tradition of prayer and study. It is also rooted in our tradition of common life. *Our common life is our primary form of preaching and the place where we are first challenged to live justly.* How we live together as brothers, at the level of our local or our provincial community, and how we share our lives as equals with our sisters in the Dominican family, will reveal whether we live the gospel or only desire to proclaim it.

Justice is not easy to preach. Justice is not easy to teach. Justice is not easy to live or to do. But just we must become — as signs in our world of the justice that God wants. Our hearts burn for justice because of our love for the God who loves justice.

Justice is the fruit of evangelization. Evangelization is the fruit of contemplation. If we want justice, we must root ourselves deeply in God, the God of the poor. We must put first things first: love of God and thus solidarity with the poor.

Where do we begin? With the first stage of evangelization suggested above: announcing the real presence of the risen Christ in our midst.

Let us pray for the gift of Dominican contemplation, the grace of Dominican preaching, and the Dominican thirst for justice.

With love, your brother,
Don

14, Salvific Preaching, Mission, and Doing Theology[1]

Twenty-five years ago, the Second Vatican Council promulgated its pastoral constitution on the church in the modern world, *Gaudium et spes.* How much has changed for all of us in these past twenty-five years! How much has changed around the world in just this past year! In Europe, Russia, South Africa, and Central America, to name only several places of tremendous change.

Last year we celebrated fifty years as a province. How many of you were members of the province, or in formation for the province, in 1939?

Now, how many of you were members of the province, or in formation, in 1965 when *Gaudium et spes* was promulgated? Next, you are going to have to project your own life span. How many of you can expect to be living members of the province in twenty-five more years, in 2015? How many of you may be here when the province celebrates its first centenary, in fifty more years, in 2039?

As we can see, history, tradition, and newness are always being woven together. This year we celebrate twenty-five years of *Gaudium et spes.*

Next year, a hundred years of *Rerum novarum.* The following year, five hundred years since Columbus set sail from Spain. And where will the province be in 2005, just fifteen years from now? And how do we get there? That is what I would like us to reflect on today.

THE SALVATION OF SOULS

St. Dominic established an Order of Preachers that he clearly intended to be an order of preachers. During the past twenty-five years, since the close of the Vatican Council in 1965, the Order and the Province have re-appropriated our identity as preachers. The Council itself instructed us, as religious, to pursue three tasks: (1) to study, retrieve, and return to the charism of our founder, (2) to root ourselves in the gospel, and the paschal mystery of the life, death, and resurrection of Jesus Christ, and (3) to adapt to the demands of our period of history (*Perfectae Caritatis,* 1965, par. 2). Jesus Christ and Dominic Guzman were thus to be our two guides through a journey of renewal as we attempted to determine what it means to be Dominican in our world, in our culture, in our period of history.

1. An Address to the Provincial Assembly: June, 1990.

To some degree we have accomplished these three tasks given us by the Council. As a Dominican family, we have reflected carefully on the life and charism of Dominic and the early history of the Order. We have often returned to the christological roots of our life and mission, with renewed biblical, theological, liturgical, and sociological awareness. We have been seriously attentive to modern culture and history.

Jesus and Dominic had at least one primary concern in common: their explicit awareness of a mission to preach. As Jesus says in the first chapter of the Gospel of Mark: "Let us go to the neighboring villages so that I can preach there also, for that is why I have come" (Mk 1:38). And our Fundamental Constitution, quoting the Primitive Constitutions, states:

> For the Order of Friars Preachers founded by St. Dominic is known from the beginning to have been instituted especially for preaching and the salvation of souls. Our brethren, therefore, according to the command of the founder must conduct themselves honorably and religiously as people who want to obtain their salvation and the salvation of others, following in the footsteps of the Savior as evangelical people speaking among themselves or their neighbors either with God or about God. (The Book of the Constitutions of the Order, 1, II)

There is another point that connects Dominic to Jesus: their concern for salvation. In response to Zacchaeus' conversion, Jesus proclaimed, "Today salvation has come to this house" (Lk 19:9). And Dominic clearly saw preaching as connected with salvation, as we saw in the above text.

Thus there may be one item on an unfinished agenda after these past twenty-five years. Dominic established the Order "for the salvation of souls." To how many of us is this an intelligible, inspiring and urgent challenge? Yet I am convinced of the importance of the phrase: "for the salvation of souls." Without it, our lives and our preaching have as much meaning as selling shoes to Imelda Marcos. There is no real need, and no ultimate significance. We may assume our importance or presume the value of the gospel, but without this phrase, what we do or who we are really makes little difference. For Dominic, "preaching and the salvation of souls" is one intrinsically connected mission, which says something about his own theology of preaching. Preaching, to be preaching, at least to be Dominican preaching, must be salvific.

The difficulty in making this expression meaningful for us has less to do with the word "salvation" than it does with the word "soul." How are we to understand these words today? I am not setting aside the traditional doctrines associated with the word "salvation": deification, sanctification, justification, forgiveness of sin, resurrection from the dead, redemption, and liberation. But before these words can truly be meaningful to most of the people with whom we speak today, there has to be a prior step. Something salvific must happen before the traditional understandings of salvation can be appropriated. We might say that these doctrines belong more to the ministry of catechesis and that we are concerned here with a very early stage of evangelization.

Our culture, and its socio-economic values, blocks our understanding. I wonder whether my nephews or nieces think of their need for salvation. They are very good men and women, but I wonder whether they are clear about any need for salvation. Our first-world culture tends flippantly to ask: saved from what? for what? Unfortunately, evangelical fundamentalism is successful because it is experienced by people as having answers to these questions. People could take or leave much of our preaching and it would make little difference in their lives. In fact, how many of us here are convinced that preaching can make a difference? If we did not preach, if there were fewer vocations, if the Order practically disappeared, would it make any significant difference? Would it make any *salvific* difference? Would not people ultimately be saved anyway?

Dominican preaching is salvific and liberating, whatever else it is. This is clear from the mission of Dominic. Our Constitutions state:

> That the salvific influence of our preaching can reach everyone, it is necessary not only to consider the circumstances and aspirations of those whom we address but also to establish a living relationship with them so that the updated preaching of the revealed word, the law of all evangelization, may endure especially among those who are far from the faith. (*The Book of the Constitutions of the Order*, 99, II)

Thus our mission is not simply preaching, but salvific preaching, the salvation of souls. What on earth could this possibly mean? We must begin at a fundamental level, the level of cultural analysis and critique, a basic step in preaching, the law of all evangelization. Dietrich Bonhoeffer once asked, "How do we speak about God in a world without religion?" (*Letters and Papers from Prison*, 1962, 164-65). We Preachers must also ask, "How do we talk about the salvation of souls?"

Soul is in fact a very common word in our society. Blacks have it. Their music has it. Their food has it. Joaquin, or Joaquin's parents, in the following poem almost lost his soul.

I am Joaquin
lost in a world of confusion,

caught up in the whirl of a gringo society,
confused by the rules,
scorned by attitudes,
suppressed by manipulation,
and destroyed by modern society.
My parents
    have lost the economic battle
and won
    the struggle of cultural survival.
And now!
    I must choose
        between
    the paradox of
victory of the spirit,
despite physical hunger,
        or
    to exist in the grasp
of American social neurosis,
sterilization of the soul
    and a full stomach.
(Rodolfo Gonzalez)

And we too must choose between the victory of the spirit or the loss of our soul to the North American social neurosis. Our Western, secular, affluent society needs soul. Our preaching has to tap into soul, or awaken people to the fact that there is *more* to life than the pursuit of pleasure, fame, power, and wealth. Upward mobility, a strong social value at this time in our country, especially for Catholics, even for many of us, is detrimental to the salvation of our soul. How difficult it is for a comfortable, powerful, or rich person to be saved, to have soul. What does it profit you if you gain the whole world and suffer the loss of your soul (Mt 16:26)

The degree of comfort to which we have become accustomed in our society is deadly. Our society has many ways of denying its bankruptcy, its loss of soul: drugs, addictions, workaholism, careerism, new commodities, more *things*, consumerism, casual sex, passing relationships. In our culture, when I preach, someone's soul *is* at stake. Either they will break through or remain enclosed in a system of values that suffocates the soul. As I said in my letter on evangelization this past January, evangelization of the middle class means a conversion from the values of the rich to the needs of the poor. Our preaching must be salvific at this very rudimentary level. It must enable people to see through, break through, desire to get through to their soul.

Joel Brende and Elmer McDonald report in their study of post-traumatic spiritual alienation in Vietnam veterans (Spirituality *Today*, Winter, 1989, pp. 319 ff): "They became victims of an unprecedented and totally unexpected deadening of the soul" (323-24). "Many described their loss of human sensitivity and emotional and spiritual responsiveness by saying, 'I lost my soul in Vietnam'" (325).

Alice Miller, in her analysis of what she calls "poisonous pedagogy" or destructive child rearing practices, speaks of the murder of the soul (*For Your Own Good*). This is dramatically manifest in Himmler's 1943 Posen address.

> I shall speak to you here with all frankness about a very serious subject. We shall now discuss it absolutely openly among ourselves, nevertheless we shall never speak of it in public. I mean the evacuation of the Jews, the extermination of the Jewish people. It is one of those things which is easy to say: "The Jewish people are to be exterminated", says every party member. "That's clear, it's part of our program, elimination of the Jews, extermination, right, we'll do it." And then they all come along, the eighty million upstanding Germans, and each one has his first-class Jew. Of all those who talk like this, not one has watched [the actual extermination], not one has had the stomach for it. Most of you know what it means to see a hundred corpses lying together, five hundred, or a thousand. To have gone through this and yet — apart from a few exceptions, examples of human weakness — to have remained decent, this has made us hard . . . By and large, however, we can say that we have performed this most difficult task out of love of our people. And we have suffered no harm from it in our inner self, in our soul, in our character (*For Your Own Good*, 79-80).

Now you may think that my use of "soul" is far removed from its biblical or theological meaning. But I suspect not. We are up against the wire in our present culture as to whether we can save our souls or not. And if we thought that we could actually help our brothers or sisters or nephews or nieces or friends or parishioners or students or counselees reach, retain, save their souls, would this not be an urgent task? Would our preaching not become salvific? Not just idle words? A whole new life would be opened up.

Preaching requires social analysis and cultural critique if the gospel is to be proclaimed. We must be able to affirm that which is good in our culture but also indicate the seeds of destruction. The number-one danger in our current renewal of religious life is the danger of being co-opted by our culture and false social values.

Are our preaching and our ministries salvific in the way that we are discussing? We must also ask this question of the way we live. Our Dominican way of life, our witness, who we are, is the primary way in which we all preach. If the gospel does not touch our souls, if it does not affect *our* lives, we can hardly expect our proclamation of the gospel to do better for others than it has done for us.

Is community life salvific for us? It can be to the degree that we embrace it generously. I am not suggesting that it is easy, pleasant, or all that it can be. I am only suggesting, if we give ourselves to the challenges of common life, that this will be one more way of preventing the negative impact of a culture from taking complete hold of us. Community life and a sense of the brotherhood help us to save our souls. We can all fantasize about life in an apartment, or with a wife or family or lover or friends, with our own income and an excellent salary, and there it is: false social or financial values taking hold of us.

Sometimes we think that there is a great division among us, an older generation and a younger generation, or however we divide ourselves up. The reality is that we all have one fundamental trait in common — our individualism. We simply exemplify the two different types of individualism discussed in *Habits of the Heart* (32-35). Some are utilitarian individualists, self-made men, self-reliant, typified by Benjamin Franklin. They can make it on their own if they have to, and they often prefer to do so. Others are expressive individualists, the romantic, therapeutic, me generation, typified by Walt Whitman. But beneath the surface, none of us speaks the language of community easily. Community life was intended by Dominic to be salvific. For us it must also be counter-cultural.

Our Dominican way of life is intended to be salvific for us so that our preaching may be salvific for others. The way of the Preacher is the way of common life, common prayer, communal study, collaborative preaching, and solidarity with the poor. Preaching is not a contemporary, relevant, intelligent reflection on a sacred text. Preaching is a way of life.

Preaching requires retrieving our contemplative roots, the God-experiences or experiences of the Spirit, which enable us to be authentic and constructive cultural critics, and thus salvific preachers. One of the negative effects of our society is the sense of drivenness, franticness, busyness into which we are socialized. This compulsive drivenness does not allow us time for contemplative life which experiences and understands time differently. For example, we have little time for awe. We then become less alive, less human.

We experience awe when we are confronted by God, or by human misery. First there is God, God's beauty, God's creation, God's people, which awe we experience only as contemplative people. It leads to wonder, worship, and eucharist. A second cause of awe is the awful: human pain, anguish, suffering, misery. It leads to a thirst for justice. This is a different kind of awe, but nevertheless another mystery which we cannot fully grasp.

God and human suffering are the two mysteries that our minds cannot adequately contain — and thus bewilderment, wonder, fear, reverence, awe are our human responses. We may try to control, define, or grapple with God, but in the end God remains God. So with human suffering, poverty, and brutality. Our impulse is to control or explain or rationalize them. But there remains mystery, even if we want them to be problems we can rationally or historically resolve.

The lack of quality contemplative time in our lives becomes manifest in two fundamental issues we face as a province: the need for an emphasis on contemplation, and the need for a greater proximity, solidarity, identity with the poor. And these two are closely interconnected, as are liturgy and the thirst for justice. Lack of time makes liturgy something we do rather than Someone we reverence. Liturgy ought also to instill in us the desire to be with the poor, with God's people. Celebrating Eucharist should make us thirst for justice. And vice versa, pastoral identity with people we serve, solidarity with the poor and socially marginal, should call forth from us the need to come together, to be together, and to celebrate Eucharist together.

Liturgy and justice can never be far apart, no more than God and the people of God are apart. The mystery of pain and the mystery of a crucified Savior are inseparable. They lead us to pray as Jesus taught us to pray: Loving God, may your name be held holy. May your will be done on earth. Give those most in need enough food today. Forgive us our sin as we forgive others. And do not put us to the test. Amen.

We experience salvation. Life becomes contemplative. Preaching becomes salvific. We desire to be poor as Christ was poor.

Our preaching, teaching, and pastoral ministry ought to be salvific. Our soul, the soul of those whom we serve, and the soul of our culture are in danger. We ourselves are in danger of being co-opted by the values of the rich. We are in need of salvation. This salvation partially comes from our common life, our contemplative life, and our apostolic solidarity with the less comfortable, the unpowerful, and the poor.

Let us now try to approach our pilgrimage from another angle, from an interpretation of the history of theology and our intellectual tradition.

THE HISTORY OF THEOLOGY AND SOLIDARITY WITH THE POOR

As Preachers, we can benefit from the study of monastic theology and also from a deeper awareness of the contrast between monastic theology and scholastic theology. We have roots in both theological traditions. The theology of the monasteries was traditional theology, even a continuation of patristic theology. Monastic theology developed in response to the questions and needs of a particular milieu, the monastery, in contrast to the schools, whether these were a particular monastery's external school in town, or a clerical school near the cathedral in a city, or later, the great urban university. The context or setting within which theology was done or taught made a difference to the theology itself. The differences between monastic theology and scholastic theology are simply the differences between a monastery and a school as a context for learning. It is easy to oversimplify the contrast. One source, Peter Comestor, contrasted those "who do more praying than reading" and those "who spend all their time reading and rarely pray" (Leclercq, 244). John of Salisbury characterized the men of the schools as innovators, "moderns," in contrast to the *veteres*, the ancients, the upholders of the tradition (Leclercq, 245). The scholastics were clearly modernists in the medieval world.

There is neither need nor time to go into the differences between these two different approaches to Christian theology except to advert to the fact that these approaches reflected the concerns, questions, and needs of two legitimate but contrasting contexts. Both monastic theology and scholastic theology were contextual theologies: their contexts or formative environments were different. The theology of the schools placed greater emphasis on the values of clarity, logic, and philosophy. Although dialectics played a prominent role in monastic education, it was scholasticism that established the disputation as an essential tool for learning. This form of arguing as a way to learn was characterized by St. Bernard as verbal battles, *pugnae verborum* (Leclercq, 250). The monk saw his theology as the fruit of his contemplation, and of his charity or Christian praxis, not so much of the faculty of reason. Monastic theology, like patristic theology, like the theology of Eastern Orthodoxy, could not be severed from spirituality or liturgy. A distinction between philosophical theology and mystical theology made no sense in a monastic context. The monastery, just as a school, just as a traditional Dominican studium, just as a university was and is a specific context which gives different theological results.

There is a further point to be made. Contemporary academic theology, or university theology, has its roots in, and affinity to, the scholastic theology of the Middle Ages. Granted that a modern university is quite distinct from the medieval university, and modern philosophy something altogether different from medieval philosophy, yet modern academic theology is of the same sort as scholastic theology in that its context is the same, namely, a school, a university setting, the academy. The theology *looks* different because modern and post-modern secular culture is not medieval Christian culture, and Kant and Heidegger are not Plato and Aristotle, but the underlying values formative of the theology are similar: clarity, logic, reason, philosophy, scientific knowledge.

I realize that it is an over-simplification to summarize the history of theology in two broad strokes — patristic-monastic theology; and scholastic-modern theology. But in the light of the awareness that all theology is contextual theology, the above contains a valid insight. It also helps us appreciate the shift that is taking place in theology today, similar to the shift in the twelfth and thirteenth centuries.

These different approaches to theology are not competitive. There was still room for monasticism after the emergence and development of scholasticism. So likewise the new theology of the twentieth and twenty-first centuries does not negate the continuing need for theology to be forthcoming from both monastery and university settings, the need for both contemplation and rationality in doing theology. Vis à vis newer theology, however, contemporary academic theology, in continuity with its scholastic predecessor, will be seen as fairly traditional.

The significant theological change since Vatican II comes from the context, the setting, in which theology is or will be done. Whether that be the barrio, the *communidad de base*, the ghetto, a woman's group, or a parish, the new theology is pastoral in contrast to academic or monastic. The primary setting for theology will no longer be the monastery or theological school but the people whom theology is intended ultimately to serve. Karl Rahner's philosophical theology will be seen as traditional by comparison to the liberation theology of Leonardo Boff, the feminist hermeneutics of Elizabeth Schussler-Fiorenza, the black theology of James Cone, or the South African theology of Albert Nolan, for these latter are distinctive in that they emphasize a different context within which theology ought to be done, a context neither monastic nor academic but nevertheless highly appropriate and even necessary for Christian theology. Latin American liberation theology is not just another theology alongside others. It has inaugurated an innovation in the history of the Christian tradition. Theology has located itself in the world *(Gaudium et spes)*, with the people (Lumen Gentium), pastoral in the sense that all theology ought to be, "popular", responsive to social concerns, the concerns of the people, not necessarily the concerns of scholars or monks. Whether we call the emerging theological tradition pastoral or political or social or contextual makes little difference. Theology has not undergone such a profound change since the twelfth century, and that theological shift had socioeconomic origins as well. The "new theology" of the twelfth and thirteenth centuries emerged within a new urban setting, a new social class, and new institutions for learning. The new *magistri*, or *scholares*, unlike the *claustrales* or *monachi*, lived in cities, removed from the country, where they could take an interest in the issues of business and commerce associated with the emerging middle class.

Liberation and feminist theologies must become increasingly self-critical. Yet the battles they fight will be no easier than the battles of the Aristotelians in the thirteenth century. As happened with Thomas Aquinas, some of their opinions will be condemned. But the day will come when they will be seen as valid carriers of the tradition. The shift will have come because of a new setting having been accepted in which theology will be done — among the people, with the poor, for those for whom the gospel was good news.

Contextual theology is not something new, but the context may be. The barrio, the ghetto, the parish will be theological centers in the future. This does not mean theology will not continue to be done in monasteries and schools, but theology will not be limited to these more conservative centers.

This suggestion which interprets the history of theology as having moved into a new context, and a new period in the history of theology, has brought us by way of our own intellectual and theological traditions once again to the issues of solidarity with the poor, with women, with the socially marginal, and it rightly raises questions for us.

Where should we ourselves be doing our theology today? What ought to be the context of our theology? for our preaching? If Dominic were founding an order of preachers *today*, with his perspicacity into the signs of the times, would he send his young student friars to learn theology at the university or to a barrio among the poor?

Further questions: If the context itself is formative of the nature of theological discourse, who comprises my own "community of discourse"? Whom do I allow to have a real and experiential impact on my thinking? The poor? The marginal? Women? Blacks, Hispanics, Africans, Asians or indigenous peoples? Or is my community of discourse primarily people like myself? Do I enter into theological conversation, share my faith, primarily with academics, other preachers, only women, other gays or straights depending upon my own sexual orientation, only radical progressives, or only conservatives? We must all examine the context of our preaching, our learning, our theology, our ministry, and widen the space of our tents, as the prophet Isaiah encouraged (Is 54:2). This same Isaiah also said:

> How beautiful upon the mountains,
> are the feet of one who brings good news,
> who heralds peace, brings happiness,
> proclaims salvation. (Is. 52:7)

If religious life, Dominican life, is to continue to renew itself, to be salvific for its members, and to bring salvific preaching to others, if we are to discover what it means to be religious, or Preachers, in our culture, at this period of history, we must move Dominican life both beyond the liberal mode of renewal of the past twenty-five years and beyond the efforts to re-assert a simply conservative model. We must widen the space of our tents, our understanding, our listening, our dialogue, our conflicts. We must discover a new context that frees us to seek the truth unburdened by the falsely framed ideological glasses within which we almost always pose our questions or to which we give unhealthy loyalty. The greatest danger still facing us as we attempt to fulfill the tasks given us by Vatican II is that we will be co-opted by our culture. The second greatest danger is that we will not be able to let ourselves move beyond the currently accepted ideological confines within which we are supposedly supposed to think.

Neither modern culture nor ideology is what Preachers are about. We live only for the sake of the gospel.

IN CONCLUSION

Our Province has set its apostolic priorities: preaching and evangelization, theological education and the intellectual life, peace and justice. We have also suggested the need for continuing emphasis on the common life, the spiritual life, and solidarity with the poor. The basic outlines for the direction we need to pursue are thus clear.

Sometimes asking the right questions can be more important in the long run than solving our immediate problems. Whether we begin with a critique of our culture or an interpretation of the history and direction of theology, we are pulled in the same direction: toward the uncomfortable. Thus my first question to us is: how do we prevent ourselves from being co-opted by the negative influences of our culture so that we can better proclaim the gospel of God?

Second question: what is the vision of church to which we are committing ourselves? It must be a vision that goes beyond current ideologically framed concepts. That which will hold us together, and unite us from within diverse communities and ministries, is a common vision of church and a common understanding of theology, even if these are not something we may live to see. Whether preachers, teachers, researchers, pastors, or men and women working for justice and peace — we can more and more begin to work toward a common vision of church and theology to which we are committed.

Final question: where do I need to be challenged? What in my own journey of faith needs most to be confronted if I am to save my soul? What must I let go of, if I am to participate more fully in a corporate provincial decision to preach only after having done theology as a community which has identified itself with the struggle of those less comfortable than we? What am I to let go of if I am to be more self-consciously contemplative?

These are three questions that the experience of the past five years has raised for me. I want to take this opportunity to express my gratitude to all of you for the privilege of serving you these past five years. Thank you.

Suggested Readings

Bellah, Robert, et al. Habits of the Heart, Individualism and Commitment in American Life. Berkeley: University of California Press, 1985.

Chenu, N.-D. *Nature, Man, and Society in the Twelfth Century* . Chicago: University of Chicago Press, 1968. Esp. 270-330.

Leclercq, Jean, O.S.B. *The Love of Learning and the Desire for God, A Study of Monastic Culture.* New York: Fordham University Press, 1961. Esp. pp. 233-86.

Little, Lester. *Religious Poverty and the Profit Economy in Medieval Europe.* London: Paul Elek, 1978.

Nolan, Albert. "Doing Theology within Every-day Experience: A South African Perspective", in *Doctrine and Life* 39 (April 1989), 187-99.

Schreiter, Robert. *Constructing Local Theologies* . Maryknoll: Orbis Books, 1985. Esp. pp. 1-21, 75-94.

Segundo, Juan Luis. *Faith and Ideologies* . Trans. John Drury. Maryknoll: Orbis Books, 1984..

Tracey, David. "The Uneasy Alliance Reconceived: Catholic Theological Method, Modernity, and Postmodernity." *Theological Studies* 50 (Sept. 1989), 548-70.

15, Preaching as Listening[1]

Dear Brothers,

As we celebrate the Triduum and the Easter Season, I want us to reflect on our vocation as Preachers. The General Chapter in Oakland spoke about preaching as "the priority of priorities" (ACTA, General Chapter at Oakland, 1989. n. 68, 3).

In the Acts of the recent Provincial Chapter, the prologue to the apostolic life and the apostolic priorities of the Province states:

> Preaching, which is the public proclamation of the gospel of Jesus, is the primary reason for our existence as a religious order. Therefore, preaching must permeate, inform, inspire and give impetus to everything that we are and do. Our study, our prayer, our common life and every aspect of our apostolic ministry must begin from, and be directed to, our mission of preaching (1990 ACTS, p. 17).

We need to read and re-read this prologue. It challenges us to reclaim our identity as "The Holy Preaching." It proposes a new paradigm for our self-understanding so that we all see ourselves as Preachers — whatever else we are doing.

During these last six years in provincial administration, during travels into other cultures, and amid a variety of challenging situations, I have had the opportunity to reflect frequently on our preaching mission. The prologue on preaching contains well-phrased insights. There is one in particular that I wish to emphasize at this time.

PREACHING AS LISTENING

> We need to draw on the wealth that is present in our communities, through communal discussion of the Word . . . and among those with whom and to whom we minister, through careful listening and the honest seeking of feedback (Prologue, 1990 ACTS, p. 21).

Ineffective evangelization and ineffective preaching are frequently a consequence of our inability or unwillingness to listen. Effective listening is essential to effective preaching. Listening indicates that we have something to learn and that we respect those to whom we preach. The gospel is not simply something we bring ready made into any context

1. March 24, 1991, Passion Sunday

whatsoever. Rather, it is a response from within a particular context. Before we respond, we must hear, and before we can hear, we must listen.

Preaching is not providing pre-determined answers to people's questions, nor ready-made insights formed prior to any interaction with those to whom we are sent, nor wrestling with the written text of scripture alone. Preaching emerges as God's word from within a specific context — God's word for these people at this specific time.

Listening indicates that we have something to learn from people that only they can teach us. As Preachers, we do not come as the learned ones, which does not suggest that we set our learning totally aside. Rather, as Preachers, we are both teachers and learners, learners continually learning, needing to listen before a pastoral response can be formed. We wrestle with the text, but also with the concrete context (con-text) in which or to which biblical texts speak, that which goes along with the text (con-text) and which must be addressed in order for there to be preaching.

Our reason for listening is theological. We are aware that our God is One-who-is-with-us (Gen 28:15, Ex 3:12, Is 7:14, Jn 1:14). The God of Jesus is with people, in solidarity with people. Thus God is already there with people before the preacher arrives. We do not bring God, as it were, from the outside, but help people to recognize God's presence already with them in their midst. As Matthew 11:25-26 suggests, revelation is already happening before we begin to preach. We are only one part of a process. We must hear what God is doing or has already done before we ourselves speak.

I think of the harm that we do when we enter another culture and do not make listening a priority. I think of the lack of respect we show people(s) when we unconsciously communicate that their present world is devoid of grace, that God is not already with them, that God is not who God is, namely, the One Who Is With Them. We communicate that we are the ones who have God and they once again are the have-nots. Jesus reversed this perspective and turned it around.

We cannot go into another culture without listening. Nor can we enter another racial context, address people of a different gender, or move into a different economic class without listening. Any and every group deserves to be heard before we proclaim the word. Listening itself is an act of witness and thus an act of preaching. Listening proclaims the gospel before we open our mouths. To invite people to speak, to approach them as preachers who are to be taught, this says more than any testimony to our own expertise.

Let me say that I do not dismiss at all the importance of our learning, our studies, our wrestling personally and critically with the text of

Scripture. These are necessary. But they do not constitute a readiness to speak or an authorization to preach by themselves alone. Much less does ordination by itself alone so authorize us. God ultimately commissions us when the word has been formed within us as God's response to these people, God's people.

Listening by itself is necessary but insufficient. Preaching also involves prayer, study, and communal life. Nor does preaching imply that we feed back to people what we have heard from them. God's word may well be a word of challenge to them, their values, their previous understanding. Yet God's word is still formed *as a response* to these people in this place, at this period in their lives and history. Preaching requires listening. What we eventually say and how we say it comes from our interaction with a variety of sources that help God's word to be formed in the Preacher and help to form the Preacher.

In some fashion, the medium is the message — and perhaps the more long-lasting message. How we preach says much about the gospel that we proclaim. Our attitude can belie our content. The form our preaching takes gives shape to our material and is intrinsic to it. What we preach — namely, the risen Christ, the gospel, faith, justice — is affected by the way we preach. Does our content inform our own preaching and our preaching give witness to the content?

If preaching is "the priority of priorities" in our apostolic life, then listening is the priority of priorities in the art of preaching. Listening, which is also at the heart of our vow of obedience, is something of a cornerstone for Dominican life. Listening, an art in which every Dominican ought to excel, is essential to both common life and apostolic life. During this Easter Season as we celebrate the living presence of the risen Christ with us, let us all practice this art of listening and pray for the grace of listening.

Your brother,
Don

Dominic at Prayer
"We must accept as Preachers that we are also contemplatives." (p. 48)

Artist, ALBERT CARPENTIER, OP

16, The Order's Apostolic Priorities and Preaching[*]

Dear Brothers,

We are an apostolic order. Preaching is the *raison d'être* for the Order. This was recently emphasized in the *Acts* of our 1990 Provincial Chapter.[1] It has frequently been emphasized by Damian Byrne.[2]

We know how sacred the preaching mission was to our father Dominic.[3] We came into being as an Order "for the sake of preaching."[4]

Following upon the updating required of us by the Second Vatican Council (1965),[5] in light of the ensuing revision of our own Constitutions (1968), and since the General Chapter in Quezon City (1977), the Order has consistently articulated its preaching in terms of *four apostolic priorities*. I would like to return in this letter to these four priorities. I will focus my reflections around four questions: To whom do we preach? Who preaches? What do we preach? How do we preach? As individuals and communities we can examine our apostolic lives with these four questions.

TO WHOM DO WE PREACH? THE FIRST APOSTOLIC PRIORITY

The final cause of the Order today is not simply preaching, nor even salvific preaching, but most specifically evangelization and catechesis in the context of a dechristianized world. The first apostolic priority of the Order is stated as: "catechesis in dechristianized cultures and milieux" (Quezon City, 1977, Par. 15, 5a, p. 16). The General Chapter in Avila (1986) articulated this as "a mission on the frontiers." Why we preach, although a larger question, cannot be separated from the question of "to whom we preach," or "where we preach": the "locus" or *ad quem* of our preaching.

The reality today is that of a world which is pre-Christian, non-

[*]. November 15, 1991, Feast of St. Albert the Great

1. *1990 Acts*, Prologue, pp. 17-24.

2. e.g., Damian Byrne, OP, "The Challenge of Evangelization," and "The Ministry of Preaching," in *A Pilgrimage of Faith* (Dublin: Dominican Publications, 1991), pp. 5-23.

3. M H Vicaire, *Saint Dominic and His Times* (1964 translation, London: Darton, Longman & Todd Ltd; reprint, 1989, Green Bay, WI: Alt Publishing Company), pp. 151-53, 191-95, 222-25, 308-15.

4. *The Book of the Constitutions of the Order*, Fundamental Constitution, par. II.

5. *Perfectae Caritatis* (1965), nn. 2-4.

Christian, post-Christian, and de-Christianized. This reality affects our preaching and challenges our understanding of mission. There are cultures which are not Christian, but which are by no means necessarily non-religious. Then there is the secular, to a great degree post-Christian, to a great extent atheistic or religiously indifferent world. Whichever context we consider, our world today is a world where the God of Jesus is not known.

The first apostolic priority of the Order not only calls upon us to be aware of this new context of our preaching but also to address it. To whom do we preach? For most of us in the Province our context is ordinarily still "the Christian world," although even in our schools and parishes we are up against a secularized, not deeply catechized, often spiritually deprived people. Even there, however, do we get to the heart of the matter: humanity's truly human thirst for God and our response to that thirst by preaching the God of Jesus Christ, the gospel?

This first apostolic priority recognizes the reality of our situation today as that of a world distant from the Christian faith for different reasons in different places. This reality raises questions for us:

Are we prepared and willing to undertake today's mission "on the frontiers" (Avila, 1986)? Do we prefer these new frontiers? Or do we prefer the classical context of a Christianized world and Christian culture for our preaching and ministry?

How do we speak about God in today's world? (I recall here Bonhoeffer's still important question.[6]) Who is the God whom I preach? To what degree is our God true God and to what degree an idol of our own making?

Where are the frontiers in our own midst? Do we have a profound enough awareness of the effects of secularism, capitalism, consumerism, and fundamentalism, and particularly how they effect "a quenching of the Spirit" in our own time? Even "Christians" are living in a new world. Today is not the same as yesterday, and tomorrow will not be the same as today.

Are we ourselves here in the heartland of the USA open to the multicultural reality and challenges in our midst, or do we still need to interpret reality from the vantage point of a dominant culture? [This question applies to the "cultures" in Bolivia and our mission there as well.] How do we "encounter" other cultures today? Are we not ourselves learning the gospel as we go along?

6. Dietrich Bonhoeffer, *Letters and Papers from Prison* (New York: The Macmillan Co., 1966), 162-64.

To whom are we being sent? Why an Order of Preachers today? This first apostolic priority of the Order parallels the first apostolic priority of the Province, namely, preaching and evangelization, yet helps to focus and make specific the context into which we are being called.

WHO PREACHES? THE SECOND APOSTOLIC PRIORITY

Here we have to do with the efficient cause of preaching, the agents of preaching, the Preachers, as well as the Order's traditional emphasis on learning and study and our contemporary emphasis on continuing formation — all of these in relationship to the second apostolic priority. The Oakland General chapter described this priority as "evangelization in diverse cultures"[7] but the Quezon City General Chapter described it perhaps better as "the cultural politics of the Order oriented to a philosophical and theological research about cultures, intellectual systems, social movements, religious traditions working outside historic Christianity."[8]

Who are preachers? How do you describe us? The Preacher is a man or woman of learning. This is our strength. It can also be our weakness. Yet Preachers are clearly educated women and men.

The second apostolic priority has to do with this tradition of learning. Vincent de Couesnongle spoke about it in terms of "the organization of intellectual work in the Order."[9] It relates to our own apostolic emphasis on theological education, the nature of that education, and specifically its pastoral or contextual character. What constitutes a theologically educated Preacher?

This apostolic priority has to do with the particular shape the intellectual tradition of the Order takes. This priority requires that some give themselves to research, others to social analysis, and still others to the pastoral ministry and to teaching. All of this has to do with "the cultural policy of the Order" because the intellectual work of the Order must be culture-sensitive. This second priority cannot be separated from the emphases in the first priority. Who is "learned" today?

Clearly, the policy of the Order today recognizes the importance of understanding the context of our preaching — that of religiously pluralistic, not predominantly Christian cultures of the East, or that of religiously indifferent, secularized, dechristianized cultures of the West, and so forth. Indeed, the first apostolic priority already recognizes the context

---

7. ACTA, General Chapter of Oakland, 1989, n. 68, 2, pp. 34, 37-8.
8. ACTA, General Chapter of Quezon City, 1977, n. 15, 5b, p. 16.
9. See International Dominican Information (IDI), no. 195 (October, 1982), 128.

of our preaching as significant and thus the second apostolic priority calls for a study of this context, of our world today — the policy of the Order with respect to cultures, the appreciation and study of cultures, being learned with respect to this context of culture. This second priority requires being learned in the theology of culture, varied religious traditions, and the varied situations in our world today. One can then go from the context to the content of preaching, such as the emphases on dialogue (Asia), inculturation (Africa), and liberation (Latin America).

But before we go to the content of our preaching, there is still more to say about the Preacher, the one who is sent.

The second apostolic priority emphasizes "a cultural policy" in the Order, the need for the Preacher to be culture-sensitive and thus context-sensitive, and thus the need for the Order to take a look at its own way of doing theology and theological education.

But who the Preacher is also requires the response: one who is continually being formed. The whole area of continuing formation is something to which I will turn in my next letter to the Province. Here I only indicate its importance. The Preacher is culture-sensitive, one who listens. The Preacher is also one who is continuously being formed, and frequently by the context of his or her preaching and ministry.

Who preaches? Men *and* women. The "cultural policy" of the Order also requires that we be gender-sensitive. "Women's issues" are not the issues of women only; they are our issues as well; they are human issues. Who should be doing more in our church today to promote women preachers than the Order of Preachers? Who should be doing more to address these issues than the church in the United States where these issues have become more clearly focused? Thus we should see the promotion and formation of women preachers and women preaching as particularly incumbent upon our Province. In a particular way this is our responsibility, and especially when it comes to the promotion of Dominican women preaching. This flows from the cultural policy of the Order, which also requires that we here in the United States give special attention in our research to issues of gender and sexism as well as race, class, and environment.

Finally it must be said that culture-learned, continuously being formed, women and men Preachers are not the only nor even the most significant agents of evangelization. The people are. Ultimately they are the preachers, the witnesses, the subjects of history, the agents of proclamation. We do not preach to them but with them. As I said in a previous letter, the first act of preaching is listening. This too flows from the cultural policy of the Order: recognizing the dignity of people as at the heart of the gospel.

WHAT DO WE PREACH? THE THIRD APOSTOLIC PRIORITY

We now leave the context and move to the content of our preaching, the material cause so to speak. The third apostolic priority of the Order is that of peace and justice, which does not describe the sum total of our preaching but does directly relate to what needs to be preached in our world today.

Simply put, what we preach is the gospel. But what is the gospel? The gospel of God that Jesus' life, death, and resurrection so embodied? The gospel of Jesus that the four evangelists each proclaimed in his own way? In some ways the gospel *is* God. But who is the God of Jesus Christ? Who is the God whom we preach? Preaching challenges us to examine our image, experience, and understanding of God.

Our God is a God who comforts us and forgives us: a God of compassion. Our God is also a God who confronts us and challenges us: a God who calls us forth to be who we can truly be. But we must also add: *God loves justice.* God is a just God. To preach God is to proclaim justice. Justice is what God is about in the world. Peace and justice are not different from the ministry of the Word: they are ministries of the Word.

This third apostolic priority challenges our preaching and raises for us still more questions. These are some of them.

Does my preaching promote an understanding of God as one who loves justice or does it reinforce the status quo?

Granted that the Preacher is not to be involved in politics in a partisan way, do I accept that preaching has political, social, economic, and ecological implications? Can we really maintain the impression that allegiance to God has no social, political, economic, or ecological consequences?

Does my preaching promote an understanding of God as one who loves life? What does it mean to proclaim a God who is pro-life?

Does our consciousness of the poor of the world affect our preaching? If we as mendicants do not take up the cause of the poor, who will?

One of the greatest challenges facing church and society today is to be able to get beyond ideology to the gospel, to be able to refuse allowing the gospel to be defined by ideological commitments. Ultimately is my allegiance in preaching to the left? the right? or to the gospel? Thus again: who/what is this gospel?

What do we do for the promotion of women in our church? Do we still attempt to maintain that these are not issues of justice? Do we actually believe that God has a bias toward men?

We do not preach a particular political agenda, nor use the power of preaching to promote a particular ideology, nor allow ourselves to become single-issue people, and yet we must be challenged as to how often or whether, if ever, our preaching is prophetic. We can think here of examples like Francisco Vitoria and Bartolomé de Las Casas. The work of Vitoria exemplifies better the second apostolic priority and the work of Las Casas the third. Do we see the inseparable connection between these two priorities? Preaching flows from theology and theology is affected by preaching. How as a Preacher do I continue to do theology today?

I repeat that this third apostolic priority does not define for us the whole content of our preaching — but it does radically and directly affect that content. It raises the ultimate theological question: Who is our God?

Thirteenth century priorities: 15 August, 1217 Dominic disperses most of his small band to different apostolic and academic locations.

(See Letter 16.)

Artist, MARY GRACE, OP

HOW DO WE PREACH? THE FOURTH APOSTOLIC PRIORITY

Here we come to the question of the form or shape our preaching takes. Undoubtedly our own individual preaching as well as the preaching of the Province takes a variety of forms: as a team, on a parish mission, in the classroom, through writing, in the context of a retreat or conference, the homily, witness, etc., etc.

The fourth apostolic priority, however — the modern means of social communication — raises a very challenging question for us. Does at least *some* of our preaching utilize the electronic media?

It is banal to say that we are no longer an oral culture nor even a print culture. We live in an electronic age.

This by no means suggests that we set aside forms of oral and written communication and proclamation. However, does our preaching recognize the reality that ours is a new age, a new world, with respect to the means of social communication? Even radio and television are not seen as modern by the young. How to preach to our people in our cultures at our period of history is an urgent question. What portion of our ministry of the Word uses these modern forms? *The Church in the Modern World (Gaudium et spes)* is a document that needs to be integrated into our style of preaching as well. Indeed, it may be this last apostolic priority which will challenge us the most. What forms do my ministry of the Word take?

And once again, this fourth apostolic priority does not stand isolated by itself but relates to each of the others as well. To what degree does the content of our preaching reflect upon the mass media, the value system inculcated through the media? The media create the world in which we live and breathe. Can we both respect the media and at the same time offer critique? The media represent a system as powerful as any political system or economic system. How do the media promote justice? Do they?

The second apostolic priority calls upon us to utilize the fullness of our intellectual tradition and put it at the service of cultural analysis. Can this be done apart from analysis of the media? Our biblical scholars, theologians, and moralists must help us here. Media ethics is an undeveloped and yet urgently important field.

We as Preachers are being continually formed ourselves by the electronic media. How can continuing formation alert us to the pros and cons of these electronic forms of formation?

The question "to whom do we preach?" raised in our reflection upon the first apostolic priority will partly be answered by how we preach.
Your brother, in St. Albert,
Don

17, The Continuing Nature of Formation[1]

Dear Brothers,

As people called to live the apostolic common life, there are two questions which we must continuously ask ourselves and the Province: (1) How healthy and effective is the apostolic life of the Province? and (2) How healthy and holy is our common life? I focused on the first area last November for the feast of Saint Albert as I called to mind the four apostolic priorities of the Order. In this letter, as we prepare to celebrate the Easter Season, I ask us to reflect upon our common life. In the concrete, this means thinking through the role of continuing formation in our lives.

WHAT IS CONTINUING FORMATION?

The official documents of the Order (*The Book of Constitutions of the Order*, Acta, *Ratio Studiorum Generalis*) speak about *formatio permanens*. We have chosen not to translate this as "permanent formation." We probably chose the translation "continuing formation" by way of contrast to the very common expression "continuing education." Yet, in doing so, something may be lost in the notion of *formatio permanens* and we might think primarily of things we do analogous to modules of continuing education. "Continuing formation," however, is a question of *our attitude toward the nature of religious life itself.* Formation is at the heart of religious life. In one sense it *is* religious life. It is the awareness that spiritual and religious life is a continuous or life-long project, never a product or goal achieved. "Continuing formation" is really an understanding of formation as continuous. Perhaps *formatio permanens* is better translated as "continuous formation" (lifelong) .

Initial formation is simply the initial phase of a life-long religious commitment that is continuously formative of who we are. Continuing formation is not then the *next* phase. Religious life is formative and all formation is continuous. Continuing formation develops within us an attitude toward life in general and religious life in particular: that we are continually being formed.

Formation as continuous suggests that it is the stuff of life itself that most fundamentally shapes us. Formation as continuous is associated with conversion, *metanoia*, and renewal, but equally significant is the ordinary daily routine of life which forms us into the people we are going

1. Easter, April 19, 1992.

to be. Although sabbaticals, renewal programs, rehabilitation programs, and educational programs are at particular times in our lives extremely important, they are secondary. The primary element in formation is the ordinary context in which I live my life. This particular context may at times be aided by some particular renewal programs where I am given the freedom to catch up, so to speak, in some area of my life that I have been neglecting. But the primary formative element in family life is the family context itself. What then are some of these elements in life-long formation?

FORMATION AS CONTINUOUS: PRIMARY INGREDIENTS

I wish to name some significant but ordinary ingredients of formation.

1. *Community.* I have come to believe that there is nothing more important in formation than the communal context in which we live. This fact challenges our communities to be as good as they possibly can be since our communities may well be the most formative elements in our lives. This fact challenges us to make our communities healthy, wholesome and spiritual. Continuing formation is first and foremost therefore the formation of community. When community life doesn't function properly, remedial programs become necessary. We should not look only outside ourselves for programs of continuing formation but to our life together itself as the source of continuous conversion, growth, and renewal. If we neglect this area of formation we may as well set the others aside. Those who necessarily live apart from a Dominican community ought still to be closely connected to one. At least half our efforts in continuing formation ought to be placed on community formation — the most immediate context within which we live our lives.

2. *Friends.* Friends are not an obstacle to community but complement community. Healthy relationships with those who are not our brothers or sisters are also an essential ingredient of religious life. A healthy community and true friends do not oppose each other. Both have a significant and formative role in our lives. I am as concerned for a person who lives in community but has no friends as for someone who has many friends but does not give himself to community. At times our friends form us more than any factor in our lives. Hence we need to choose friends wisely and choose friends who value religious and celibate life. I have written before on the relationship between brotherhood and friendship (Letter No 9).

3. *Ministry.* Equally formative for us, and obviously so, is our ministry. We are profoundly formed, humanly and spiritually, by what

we do, to whom we minister, the challenges from those we serve. Ministry is obviously a central issue in an apostolic spirituality. Hence we need to make wise decisions about ministry. But there is also reason to allow ourselves to be challenged about ministry so that we grow and deepen. As Isaiah says, "Widen the space of your tents" (Is 54:2). I think here again of my previous letter on the apostolic priorities of the Order. To what degree do I allow these priorities to form me? To what degree do I allow those to whom I minister to form me? Do I enter a ministry as if already formed (contrary to the notion of formation as continuous) or am I open to learning? How well do I listen?

4. *Prayer.* Along with community, friends, and ministry, prayer stands out as equally significant. How we pray can vary; that we pray is essential. How do you pray? It seems as certain as anything to me that a religious who does not pray is not continuing his or her formation. They are opening themselves to stagnation, resentment, and the lack of resources to overcome disappointment and sustain hope.

Both intense personal prayer and common liturgical prayer are essential. Common prayer is an essential element of common life. It says something about who we are. The reality in the Province is that those communities in the Province who have the best prayer life are also the best communities. But common prayer alone is insufficient. We all need our own personal ways of being with God and these vary. The annual retreat is certainly high on the list. How do we sustain God's presence and our awareness of that presence without taking time to advert to that presence or to be more present to God?

The celebration of the Eucharist also contributes to our prayer, but, for the ordained, the Eucharist is never intended to be the priest's personal prayer or devotion. The Province experimented a year ago with inviting some of the brethren to do a retreat together — to pray, preach, and play together. I hope this continues. But not only retreats, our regular rhythm of awareness of God is what helps to form us.

5. *Self-reflection.* As we know from our study of philosophy, the unexamined life is not worth living. A certain reflectiveness, not an excessive introspection, is necessary to a life which is being continuously formed. One of the greatest satisfactions in religious life is to see older men who are alive — intellectually, emotionally, spiritually. And a great sadness is to see others who long ago seemingly ceased to grow. Youth is indeed not a question of chronological age but an attitude of mind and disposition of soul.

Most of us, at some point, reach a crossroad in life. It occurs at different points for different people. But it is one of the major turning points in life.

Which road we take gets determined: either we become people of gratitude or people of resentment. It depends to a great degree on how we handle the disappointments of life. Either we take an attitude of acceptance and resignation, seeing suffering and setbacks as opportunities, or an attitude of feeling cheated by life and treated unfairly. We seek justice on earth. Yet for many life is still not fair. Ultimately justice is what God works out. How we reflectively and gracefully handle our disappointments in life profoundly affect the people we will become. This is formation — who we are choosing to be.

6. *Significant Events.* There are clearly some events in our lives which take on greater significance in our formation than others. How we respond to these events or integrate them will make a major difference. I can mention several examples from my ministry as Provincial: my cross-cultural experiences in the trips to Bolivia, Central America, Nigeria, and the Philippines; living with one of the brothers and sharing his struggle with AIDS; certain specific occasions for preaching, such as professions. Previously I could point to some of the extended retreats I have made at Christ in the Desert Monastery. More recently there have been the experiences of loss and grief: someone's decision to leave, an unexpected death, my mom's death and the continuing sadness it brings. These events and people are very much part of who we are. We are not individuals who can be defined by ourselves alone. We are a network of relationships and are genuinely defined by others who are literally part of us. Likewise we are our experiences. Someone once asked me whether I thought I would be a celibate religious today if I had never had asthma as a child. Given the significant role it played in my early life, I would have to say that I would not be the person I am today without that experience. There might be another person with the same name but not the person I presently am. We can all name some of these formative events in our lives.

7. *Learning.* Materialists have maintained that we are what we eat. We might also argue that we are what we read, what we listen to, what we watch on television. Clearly we are what we learn, and learning has a strong and significant history in the Order. Here I would like to raise some further questions for us. When does learning stop in our lives and why do we ever reach a point when we think we have no more to learn? How do we learn? From books only, from people only, from our own experiences only? What does it mean to be a "learned" Preacher today? I raised a similar question in my letter last November when reflecting on the second apostolic priority of the Order — the particular pastoral, contextual, and multicultural character of the Order. Formation as continuous implies a

continuous learning — a love of learning, and an awareness of the variety of loci in which learning takes place. Learning is not exclusively rational. From whom do I learn? Am I willing to expand my community of discourse? Do I have deep discussion only with those whom I intuit as agreeable to me? Can I allow my deeply held pre-convictions to be challenged? Is my ultimate allegiance intellectually to the right or the left or the gospel? Is fuller intellectual conversion still possible for me? Is it presently happening?

Recently at our conference on doing theology contextually, we became aware of how important theology is for us as Dominicans, how formative it is, and how we need more consciously to do theology contextually, contemplatively, and communally. We do not learn in isolation from each other.

8. *The Unfamiliar.* Over twenty years ago I read a book on synectics. One of its major principles was to make the strange familiar (analogy helps here) and the familiar strange (thus jarring us as parables do into some realization of meaning). As we mature, one of the obstacles to our continuing formation is that we prefer the familiar, we feel at home with familiar surroundings and routines, we do not allow our personalities to be stretched. This is unfortunate. The unfamiliar may in fact be one of the greatest avenues to continuing formation. We all need the familiar. We all need continuity. But sometimes we are simply too resistant to life in another community, or style of community, or geographical location, or ministry, when all of these can be so enriching for us. We choose to live narrow and deprived lives. I have mentioned on other occasions the need to widen the spaces of our tents, or to open ourselves to being bilingual and bicultural, or to examine the context of our preaching and theology. What does itinerancy mean for us today? How do we allow ourselves to be stretched? These are the questions and issues central to seeing life as a continuous process of formation. We must at times open ourselves to the unfamiliar, to the stranger, or to the context in which I am not the expert and am required to change roles.

9. *Leisure.* As religious we are not supposed to be a leisure class. At the same time neither is the witness of our lives supposed to allow workaholism to masquerade as virtue. This is a very difficult balance to maintain. There are clearly men in the Province who I wish would take more time for themselves, their communities, their friends, or their prayer. But there are others at times who strike one as genuinely lazy, unmotivated, with little drive at all. How difficult a balance it is to achieve! I want to emphasize that regular leisure is a form of continuing formation. Ministry without an appreciation for the values of leisure, play

and humor suggest someone so driven that we need (and thus probably manipulate) those to whom we minister more than they need us. We need to put our own importance in perspective. We can easily be led to exaggerate our self-importance. We become driven to succeed. Then once again we have less and less space and time for God and grace. There need to be times when we give witness to the awareness that the future is not in our control.

10. *Preaching.* Our deepest identity is that of a Preacher. It is in the act of preaching that we are most who we are. Like community, there is really nothing more formative of us. Hence the need to give attention to the context, content, and form of our preaching. Also the need for us to have fora where we can preach to one another — such as in community or on retreats — if this is truly when we are most who we are. Also then the need for us to allow our preaching to be challenged and for us to have structured ways of receiving feedback. We should be asking: how am I as a preacher changing? What structures have I developed for listening to and hearing from those to whom I preach? Do I see preaching at the core of my spirituality and religious identity and how can I deepen that identity? Do I live what I preach? As friars and Preachers, community and preaching are the primary and ordinary sources of our continuous formation.

TRANSITIONAL FORMATION

Christian life and religious life are intended to be continuously formative. In Dominican life we refer to the first phase in this process of continuous formation as initial formation, analogous to how Christian formation celebrates the rites of Christian initiation. Another important aspect of continuous formation is the experience of transition. In 1990 the Province, in its own *Ratio Formationis Particularis,* began to use the expression "transitional formation." The wider church analogously celebrates liturgically and recognizes the importance of transitions in Christian life.

These transitions in Dominican life can be of varied kinds. I allude to some of them here in order to call our attention to them. Each deserves further comment by itself. After initial formation, much of our formation will be transitional formation. We as brothers and as a Province need to give more attention to these transitions.

We have discovered and discussed that the transition from initial formation to and through the first community and ministry of assignment is critical. It is a genuine phase in formation with its own issues, crises, and adjustments. It involves both a welcome and also painful engagement with the wider life of the Province. It is as significant a period as is initial formation.

There are the transitions from one ministry to another, one community to another, or both. During these I have discovered how truly fragile many of us are. These transitions often surface issues unattended to or set aside in a previous ministry or community. Often these can be mid-life issues. We need to do far better in giving attention to the formative aspects of these transitions in our lives.

Aging and the transition to limited service is another area of transitional formation requiring great attention. As we move into these years, our spiritual lives should blossom and flourish. How attentive are we to the spiritual, emotional, intellectual, social, and physical aspects of this transition? We want to be sure that the messages we give to our men going through this phase of transitional formation are ones of love, care, pride, and concern.

We can begin to see more and more how truly continuous is formation and how multi-faceted it is. When we speak of a transition as formative, we recognize it as an opportunity for human and spiritual growth. We are talking about our lives of faith.

Not only do individual brothers go through transitions, so do communities and apostolates. Every time a brother leaves a community or moves into a new community, that community becomes a new community. And how many of our apostolates are the exact same apostolates they were ten years ago? Transitions are a major part of our lives and a significant part of formation. How do we prepare for them? Can we embrace them? Do they deepen us or destroy us?

As I said in the beginning of this letter, *formatio permanens* is a question of an attitude toward the nature of religious life itself. This attitude cannot be legislated but it can be promoted. Formation as lifelong is an attitude we are all called upon to promote and exemplify.

Where I will be personally and spiritually by the end of 1992 depends to a great degree on you, my brothers. I do not always welcome your challenges. I am deeply grateful for your love and support. I too am very much in the process of being formed by my community and by the brotherhood, by my friendships and commitments, by my ministry of leadership, by prayer and self-reflection and spiritual direction, by the very significant events of this year, by trying to be a learning teacher, by remaining open to the new and unfamiliar and unexpected, by doing better at leisure and being less driven by work, and by my opportunities to preach.

In the risen Christ,
Don

18, The Vow of Poverty[1]

Dear Brothers,

As we celebrate the feast of St. Catherine of Siena, I have pondered what to call to our attention. It was not difficult to decide to return to the vow of poverty and its continuing challenge.

SIMPLICITY OF LIFE

Vowed poverty requires of each of us a simplicity of life. Simplicity, however, is not easily prescribed. It admits of individual differences. The biblically-based, Augustinian, and socialist axiom applies: from each according to their ability; to each according to their need.

But "need" has become an ambiguous concept in modern, capitalist, and consumer societies. We easily stretch it to suit what we want to justify. Yet vowed poverty raises a haunting and constant question: is this necessary?

Vowed poverty also raises other challenging questions: Is something necessary only in order to make my life more comfortable? To how much comfort am I entitled? Discomfort in itself is not a virtue, but what norm can I use to determine how much comfort is too much? We are probably all somewhat ill at ease with the degree of comfort to which we have become accustomed. Have we religious actually become accustomed to a degree of comfort higher than our lay counterparts? Would our lay peers consider us to be living "comfortable lives" rather than "simple lives"? Is the gospel something we use to advance our own professional identities or is it that foundational reality to which we strive to conform our lives?

Most of us probably do live simply — relatively speaking; relative to other privileged classes in advanced capitalist societies, but not relative to others throughout the world. Do we see ourselves as people of privilege and do we have a certain sense of entitlement about the privileges to which we have become accustomed? Is privilege something we are willing to let go of?

THE COMMON LIFE

Ultimately, and minimally, the vow of poverty expresses commitment to the common life. As with each of the vows, it expresses a willingness to be dependent upon the brotherhood. This is perhaps the most difficult

1. April 29, Feast of St Catherine.

aspect of the vow. We live in cultures, societies, and periods of history that glorify independence, self-help, and autonomy.

Yet such societies do not give our lives meaning. They do not create conditions that are conducive to human care. They falsely create the illusion that maturity comes from a capacity to compete, from self-sufficiency, from defining ourselves over against each other rather than in relationship to each other. We become disconnected, isolated, centers of exaggerated self-importance. We see ourselves as centers with the world revolving around us. Individuality is prized at the expense of the common good.

We must admit that religious life has been profoundly affected by this attitude. Does not the good of the individual self too often take precedence over the struggle to live shared, common values? Does not self-fulfillment hold a priority over self-sacrifice? Naturally these values need not be in conflict with each other, but they often are. Which then holds the stronger sway over us? If we are honest, do we not resist a community's encroachment on our preferred style of life?

And yet is our witness to the common life not what we most have to offer our society? Is it not supposed to be our primary form of preaching? Is it not what is most counter-cultural about who we are? The common life does not mean simply living under the same roof. Many people do that. Rather it says something about the quality of our commitment to each other, our willingness to speak the truth to each other, genuine care for one another's well being, genuine diversity worked out fraternally where there remains space for disagreement. Common life means that I think first of "we" and only then of "me".

SOLIDARITY

A life of vowed poverty is not something we choose "for ourselves alone." The more committed we are to a simple life and the common life, the more we realize that our lives are closely interwoven with those of others. Poverty is woven into the total fabric of our lives which are intended to give witness to the gospel and make our preaching credible. Vowed poverty connects us to a world wider than our own. This is expressed by the word "solidarity".

Pope John Paul II talks about solidarity, as do basic Christian communities in Latin America. Solidarity is one shape that a thirst for justice takes in our period of history. It is also the shape that our vow of poverty must take. The word "poverty" today suffers from the fact that "evangelical poverty" is so disconnected from the harsh economic realities of the poor. The increasing and gradual disassociation of these two, with concomitant rationalization, leads to a poverty perceived as hypocrisy. How else can the world understand it?

We can only put an end to the erosion of our witness through the concrete practice of solidarity with the poor. As a Province, as communities, and as individuals, we must continue to struggle with how to be in solidarity and take concrete steps in this direction. This is something for which we need to be held accountable. Our life together will be enriched by solidarity. So will the quality of our witness, the content of our preaching, the integrity of our lives, and the bonds that bind us together. Solidarity can motivate us to live simple lives and help us to appreciate and understand common life.

STEWARDSHIP

Another important dimension of the vow of poverty is that of stewardship. We are called to be responsible stewards of that which has been given to us. We neither live nor minister on the basis of our own earnings alone. The far majority of our revenue, without which we could not survive, comes from benefactors, bequests, funding literally entrusted to us with a sacred trust. The people, including the poor, trust us to be good stewards of all our resources — financial, human, property, talent, health. To live poverty is to live at the hands of others, and to be accountable to them for a wise use of the resources entrusted to our care.

The United States bishops recently wrote their pastoral letter highlighting this fact of stewardship. We expect stewardship from laity in the church and from bishops. To what degree do we require it of ourselves? Would we ourselves give from our widow's mite to an organization that used its resources as we do or lived as we do? I do not expect a yes or no answer to this question. Rather I am concerned that we see it as a significant question.

The vow of poverty not only calls us to a simple life. Simple living can still be individualistic living. Rather poverty calls us to a corporate identity, to a sense of being in something together as brothers, to a common good that goes beyond my personal individual well being, to a common life among us as friars and a solidarity with people that extends far beyond the brotherhood alone. Both this common life and this solidarity with the poor and marginalized of the earth require a commitment to being good stewards. For this we will be held accountable, not only as individuals but as a Province. Vowed poverty is ultimately a freely chosen radical accountability. It is this accountability to each other and to others that vowed poverty forces us to address and never allows us to escape.

MENDICANCY

Vowed poverty also raises the issue of mendicancy — an idea not easily interpreted in our period of history. We do not like to think of ourselves as beggars. Yet, in fact, begging is to a great degree the economic basis of our lives.

There are modern forms of begging that we do through our fundraising and development efforts. Also, at times, we assume that begging should be the task of only a few rather than the responsibility of all of us. Mendicancy today raises two questions in particular.

1. Are we too proud, too sophisticated, to see ourselves as beggars? Again it is a question of our identity. One of the most serious dangers and challenges facing religious life in the United States lies here. Are we all going to be required to be major income producers so that this fact alone will destroy any solidarity with the poor or possibilities for subsidizing or sustaining creatively significant apostolates? Will we be reduced to being no longer of service to society (the reason for tax-exempt status) because all we can do is sustain our own quality of life?

2. Is a self-identification as mendicant in conflict with the reality of how we live? Mendicancy morally requires simplicity of life. All of these fit together as a whole: a simple life, common life, solidarity with the poor, good stewardship, and being mendicant. Is mendicancy a workable concept in modern, post-industrial, capitalist societies? Are mendicants entitled to the quality of health care presently available to us? Would a mendicant have difficulty thinking of himself as "on welfare" in a modern welfare society? Is such beneath our dignity? Are those with higher salaries more prized members of a community? Should we simply admit that we no longer are mendicant or is the struggle with this dimension of our history one of the struggles that will help us to move beyond the current prevailing liberal models of religious life? What shape should mendicancy take among us today?

As friars, we are not simply an apostolic religious order. We are mendicants. How do we balance and struggle realistically with our financial resources, real financial needs, the quality of our lives, and the extent of our hospitality and generosity toward others?

IN CONCLUSION

There are clearly many questions which the vow of poverty raises. None of us has the answers to them. But certainly these are important questions with which we must struggle — personally, communally, as a Province, as an Order. While the vow of poverty does not require that we live lives of economic deprivation, nor even a pseudo frugality that makes us inhospitable, stingy, and often falsely proud, the vow of poverty does have something to say about the value system of our world and the degree to which we accomodate ourselves to it. Poverty is a freely chosen alternative way of life rooted in the gospel.

Happy feast of St Catherine,

Your brother,
Don

19, Dominican Poverty:
a Somewhat Radical Reflection[1]

MARY ELLEN BUTCHER, OP

Religious in our day are being asked to re-imagine, to re-image, to renew, to refound their orders, their communities, their way of life itself. It is significant that all of these tasks, all of these verbs, begin with "re". The project does not start from scratch. It moves, rather, as do all human projects, from the known to the scarcely perceived, from the experienced to the unfamiliar, from what is to what can be. Vision presupposes memory.

We Dominicans enter into the re-imaging process with our own family album of memories captured in word and fresco, in wood and stone and bronze. These images speak to us of the dream that captured us in the beginning, the dream that we would send forth to capture others in a half-guessed future time.

One such memory is embodied in McGlynn's sculpture of Dominic on the campus of Providence College. It portrays an intense Dominic rushing to the preaching with a momentum barely held in place by the solid bronze. It is the same Dominic that Vicaire gives us in words, a Dominic traveling with haste and with unmitigated enthusiasm down the roads of Europe, unperturbed in the face of opposition, of physical hardship, of death itself.

Similarly, through Suzanne Noffke's translation of Catherine's *Letters*, we come in contact with a woman reaching out with great urgency to persons of every walk of life. The *Letters* show her haste to bring the message of First Truth and the power of Christ's Blood to reform the Church and the Order, to bring peace to the cities, to renew her world while she still had time.

People in a hurry cannot afford to be burdened with excessive baggage. People consumed by God and the work of God do not need to secure themselves with possessions. Dominic and Catherine were both

1. The following article, written by Sister Mary Ellen Butcher, OP, was sent by Fr Goergen with letter number 18, on "The vow of poverty". His purpose, as he put it, was to "stimulate further reflection on the vow of poverty," adding that the article was "written [in 1990] while she was the executive director of the National Association of Treasurers of Religious Institutes," and that "her untimely death last year remains a great loss. "

clearly conscious of the importance of this for themselves and for their followers. Out of this consciousness, they urged their disciples to embrace a poverty that would be voluntary for the sake of the mission.

Out of the memory of their urgency comes our call to re-image Dominican poverty. It is a call heard in different ways by all religious. In our day poverty is perhaps the most enigmatic of the vows. What does it mean? What can it mean for us as Dominicans in this time and place?

We live in a society in which extremes of wealth and deprivation dominate the scene. In our cities, large and small, we find the unemployed, the homeless and the refugee living on the very streets where power is exercised and wealth generated. What does our vow of poverty mean in the context of this society?

We are part of a Church which has proclaimed its preferential option for the poor, a Church which struggles with its own landed wealth, with its own dependence on the generosity of the rich and powerful, with the dilemma of how and where to allocate its resources. What does our vow of poverty mean in the context of this Church?

We are part of religious institutes in the Western world, institutes whose members are aging rapidly, whose numbers are diminishing, who are faced with the very real problem of providing for the future of their life and mission from a fundamentally inadequate earnings base. What does our vow of poverty mean in the context of this reality of religious life?

We are part of an order that has called itself mendicant, an order whose founder left a bequest of voluntary poverty to his followers as a partner to their preaching, as a sign of the authenticity, the credibility of that preaching. What does our vow of poverty mean in the context of this Dominican charism?

This article is intended as a reflection on the vow of poverty and on what it can mean to live this vow authentically in our time and place. It is a reflection which has grown out of experience and which is meant to lead to dialogue on questions such as:

What does the vow of poverty mean in my own life today?
How do we as a community deal with questions about this vow?
How do we practice it? The question is not how well, but simply how.
What are the hard questions about poverty for me? for us? What are the things we would rather not talk about?
What does poverty mean for our mission, for our ministries, especially for our ministries among the poor in the present and the future?

Communities often do find the vow of poverty and all that is related to it difficult to discuss, and all of us have our own areas of defensiveness in this regard. This reflection is offered in the belief that in the context of our world, our Church and of Dominican life today, it is important for us to let down our defenses and begin the conversation.

The reflection begins, as it must, with the Word of God. The scriptures offer us many figures of the *anawim*, the poor of Yahweh. A poignant and powerful figure, and one frequently used, is the widow. Such a widow is the one whom the prophet Elijah met during the famine.

This widow had experienced the severity of the famine and had only enough flour and oil, or so she thought, to fix one last meal for herself and her son. Elijah talked her into sharing that small substance with him and promised that if she did so she would have enough flour and oil to last through the drought. She agreed, and all happened as the prophet had said.

A second figure of the poor as widow was that one whom Jesus observed among a group of people making their contributions to the Temple treasury. Jesus noted her because he perceived that she was not just throwing something into the collection, but that she "gave all she had to live on."

There are certain commonalities between these two women. Both of them had little. Both of them gave what they did have and gave it for the common use, in trust and with, as far as we can know, a certain abandon and freedom. It is worth a moment's pause to imagine how it must have felt to have been one of those widows, to let go of the last thing you have to live on.

We know the end of the story of Elijah and the widow he met. We look back on it from a future vantage point and see that everything worked out alright, that there was a happy ending, that the widow and her son survived at least until the end of the drought. Virtue was rewarded almost at once.

It is quite different with the widow whom Jesus watched. We have no idea what happened to her, whether she met a rich widower, whether she took her place among the beggars of Jerusalem or whether she made it until her next Social Security check. We are not looking back at her whole story but are, as it were, standing together with her in her now, not knowing the outcome of her generosity. It is precisely this which makes her story more real to us, and more difficult for us. It is more like our own story, more like our own call to live out our vow of poverty.

The vow of poverty places us who profess it in the situation of those two widows. It calls us to give everything we have to live on to the common treasury, trusting that the community will provide what we need. This reciprocal giving and trusting with no holding back is the common life and it is this common life which is at once integral to our vow of poverty and a counter-cultural statement in and to our society.

This society is one whose primary values are accumulation and power. Tom Wolfe in his satirical novel, *Bonfire of the Vanities*, portrays powerfully the greed and envy which are the driving forces not only of the "masters of the universe," but of many at all places on the socio-economic spectrum. The daily newspaper reinforces the picture. Stories of young children who choose the risk of the drug trade over the security of an ordinary job are among the many stories that speak to the pervasiveness of the desire for quick wealth.

Examples can be multiplied, and for us to state in the midst of this society, "Nothing I earn is mine; nothing I receive by way of gift is mine," sounds alien indeed, sometimes even to our own ears. But the truth of the common life is just that: whether I win the lottery or am president of a university or wash cars, nothing I receive is mine. I become like the widow in the Gospel; I place it all in the common treasury.

Equally, we become like the widow in the Elijah story: we share in the common treasury. Our sharing is not dependent on our earnings but on our needs. If my sister or brother wins the lottery and I need surgery, those winnings are available for my need. If my sister or brother wins the lottery and she or he needs surgery, the availability of funds has nothing to do with the winnings but with the need. What is earned, what is received belongs to all of us and is available to each of us according to our individual need.

This understanding of the common life has a long history. In a past many of us can remember, common life seemed in many ways simpler and easier, at least easier to organize. Most of us never touched money, never knew if we had a lot or a little and really never cared. We spoke of the vow of poverty as freeing us from such cares. Our clothes, our meals, our furnishings, our entertainment were generic, and our individual earnings were irrelevant. This was the common life as we experienced it, and it was appropriate to its time and to the environment of religious life at that time.

However, religious life has changed. The world both inside and outside our communities has changed. Our manner of living the vow of poverty has changed, and thus our understanding of the common life must change as well. The process of this change has taught us many things. We have learned that religious life is a choice made not just once. We have learned that we can be and are responsible for what happens within our communities. We have learned that the individuality of the person is a gift and that neither gifts nor needs are generic. We have learned that religious life is lived in the midst of a world in need.

We have had to translate those learnings into new understandings and new ways of living all of the vows. In each case the translation has been accompanied by struggle, a struggle within each and among all, as we sought a clearer, deeper sense of meaning and direction for our commitment in the context of our charism and of our time and place.

The struggle to come to a new understanding of the vow of poverty has been intensified by our awareness of the poverty of so many in our world, so many whose lives we touch each day. The very name of the vow came into question. How could we call ourselves poor when we had so much more than those around us? Suggestions were made to rename the vow as a vow of simplicity of life, and we began an earnest search for ways to simplify our own lives.

This search for simplicity has been a significant part of our renewal. Seeking to have less in a world where more is the norm gives us a different perspective on that world, a perspective of radical critique. Reducing the clutter in our lives makes us more mobile, more ready to respond to mission. Stripping ourselves of what is not essential frees us for God and for neighbor, enables us to appreciate more deeply the simple gifts of beauty and truth and goodness.

Yet our memories of community conversations on simplicity of life, the honesty of our evaluation of our own simple living also reveal to us that simplicity is very much a matter of individual insights, preferences, values, choices and decisions. How many of our conversations have ended with, "Well, what is simplicity for you just isn't for me," or, "You say that X is a luxury, but for me it is a necessity," or, "I really do need this." How many of our conversations simply ended? The invitation and the challenge to reexamine our own choices and our own lifestyle has led to growth. However, the uneasy sense of guilt which has sometimes accompanied such conversations has probably been less productive and may have led to the defensiveness of many community discussions of the vow of poverty.

We have come a long way in discovering our need to be responsible and simple in our lifestyle. At the same time, we have become aware that we are called to more. Simplicity of life prepares the ground within us, but in itself it does not have the radical quality of the vow of poverty. It does not go to the root of our lives, the root of possessiveness, the root of independence, roots which left untended can separate us from God, from one another and even from the earth, can prevent us from living that compassion for which our world cries out to us.

We are called by the vow not just to reduce but to let go of what we possess and, in the process, to let go of our independence. We are called to discover new dimensions of poverty itself in the non-possessiveness and interdependence of the common life. The precedents are good. If the widow in the story of Elijah had held onto her flour and oil, both she and her son would have starved. If she had not cast her lot with the prophet, they would not have made it. If we are realistic about Dominican life and all religious life today, we know that the same is true of us. If we are perceptive about the situation of our Church, we know that the same is true of us. If we read with clear eyes the signs of our times and of our world, we know that the same is true of us.

How do we live the vow of poverty as common life? How do we reintroduce into our lives that radical dimension of Dominican poverty? How do we become mendicant again, for the sake of our mission, for mobility and for credibility in our preaching? What asceticism does this demand of us? I would suggest that the way in which we begin to live and to express the common life in our day is through responsible, participative and collaborative planning for the use of our resources. Thus, the asceticism demanded lies in three areas: the pooling of resources, planning and collaboration.

The pooling of resources places demands on the individual, the local community and on the larger congregation or province. For the individual, it means that whatever I receive by way of remuneration or gift — or winnings — is seen not as mine, but as common. In a sense, nothing comes to me; everything comes through me. In this way, as individuals we are more than simple, we are really poor because we have nothing. This is a hard saying. It is also a hard saying to add that for all of our needs we depend, not on our own resources, but on the common resources, that we do no individual saving. Patrimony is a special case, and the particular law of the institute deals with it. However, this view of the common life implies that patrimony is not used as an outside source of funding to enable a person to avoid depending on the community.

The common life means that local communities view their collective resources not as their own, but as part of the common resources of the larger congregation or province. This demands responsible decision-making, but it also can prevent some of the have and have-not differences among local communities which arise from different scales of remuneration.

The congregation or province is not simply beneficiary in this system. In order to make the common life possible, the larger entity has responsibility to provide for the legitimate needs of its members. If this is not done, hoarding is inevitable. The members, all of us, in turn have to accept the responsibility for evaluating our own needs, for making them known. We have to move beyond the fear of not having enough, not having what we set our heart on. The common life is not a game for those who would manipulate the system; it is an adult enterprise for those who are willing to give of themselves and to be honest to and about themselves, who are willing to be free. For this reason, the common life is an ideal, yes, but also a process of growth into a new way of viewing material resources, a new way of speaking the language of money.

It is important to remember that the common life involves far more than money, far more than material resources. As Dominicans, we have been brought up on the tradition of contemplating and sharing with others the fruits of our contemplation. We know that just as the contemplating involves the whole of ourselves, so does the sharing. All of the gifts of mind and heart that we have received in love, we are asked to give in love. Catherine speaks to this in her *Dialogue* (Ch. 2, Section 7):

> I could have supplied each of you with all of your needs, both spiritual and material. But I wanted to make you dependent on one another so that each of you would be my minister, dispensing the graces and gifts you have received from me.

In our society, money is a language by which we convey many of our values, and our pooling of resources becomes a way of stating our willingness to be community and to be free for mission. It speaks of our willingness to embrace the asceticism of holding nothing back.

This asceticism of pooling of resources leads inevitably to the asceticism of planning, a planning which is participative and which involves, in different ways, the whole of the congregation or province. Planning as an exercise of the common life means that each person, each local community, the congregation or province as a whole plan for longer periods and budget for shorter periods on the basis of an honest assessment of the needs of each and of all.

The context of this planning for us is our shared and diverse Dominican charism of preaching and teaching God's Truth. The context is also the totality of the gifts and needs, the whole human reality, of the individual members of our branch of the Dominican family. In the mystery of God's creative love we are not generic. All are called to give of their gifts to the common mission, but the call differs with the gift and with the giftedness of each person. All are called to give of their gifts, but the gift and the call differ at different stages of each one's life. Likewise, each one is enabled to receive according to the need of each. Just as the gifts differ, so do the needs vary among persons and for each person at different stages of life. In the common life, the receiving is not in the measure of one's income or resources, but in the measure that expresses the community's response to each person's need at this moment of life.

The asceticism of planning in the common life embraces both the gifts and the needs. It prompts us to come to decisions together about how we choose to use the gifts and meet the needs in ways that enable us to live our mission into the future. Planning is an asceticism embraced for mission and for life. The vow of poverty, as it calls us to live the common life and to share in the responsibility for our communities by our pooling of resources and by our planning and budgeting, creates for us an economic system that is unlike the system surrounding us. It is radically different in that it is not wealth or earnings which provide access to the benefits of the society, but rather need. It is a system in which the allocation of resources is not the result of a monetary bidding and in which accumulated wealth does not provide the basis of power. Our Dominican brother, Louis-Joseph Lebret, in his proposal for a "human economy" envisioned a new order based on meeting peoples needs. His model could indeed have been Dominican common life well lived.

What has been described so far, however, pertains to congregations or provinces individually. There is more. At our moment in the history of religious life in the Western world, there must be more. We must begin to study and prepare ourselves for the asceticism of collaboration as many have already done. Collaboration "stretches the flaps of our tents" and enables us to look around us to see who could be and should be included in our work, perhaps even in our life. Collaboration begins to redefine the common life for us, to suggest a new meaning of common, of who is included in "common."

Collaboration is indeed a discipline. It will lead us to new ways of pooling our resources, of throwing in our lot with others, of participative planning, in other words, new ways of living a new kind of common life. We will also have to learn a new set of needs, how to express them and how to meet them. Above all, collaboration will demand of us a new level of letting go.

However, the recognition that 50% of the religious communities in the US. have fewer than 100 members and 33% have fewer than 50 members gives us a sobering view of religious life. For any of us to believe we can "go it alone" at this time is either foolish or a luxury.

For us as Dominicans, collaboration may most often take the form of a family reunion. The common novitiate is an example, as are the many instances of shared ministry in parishes and schools and colleges and motherhouses throughout this country and the world. The new shape of

Dominican life, and indeed of all religious life, will include models such as these as well as shared retirement facilities and even the merger of whole congregations and provinces. In some form collaboration is an outline on all of our not-very-distant horizons. It will not be an easy road, and we will all die — a little or a lot — on the journey. Perhaps our embracing of the discipline of the common life now within our own communities can be a part of our preparation for living in a "wider tent."

A reflection on the common life is filled with hard sayings. Why undertake it then? For Dominicans, the answer is always "for the mission," for a mission rooted in that compassion which drove Dominic and Catherine and so many of our predecessors, known and unknown. Poverty, lived as the common life, prepares us for mission because it is rooted in and productive of that same compassion, for myself, for one another, for the world. I learn compassion for myself as I recognize without guilt and without denial who I am and where I am and what my needs truly are at this moment in my life's journey. With compassion as well as with honesty I also recognize the letting go to which I am called at this stage.

The common life is rooted in compassion for one another in community. Compassion sensitizes us to one another and to one another's true needs, and gives us the strength for that "tough love" for one another which is sometimes required of us. Living the common life in compassion we learn to trust one another, to trust the community, to trust enough not to hold back.

Living the common life opens us to a new compassion for our world. When we allow ourselves to have nothing, to be dependent and give over control of material resources to others, our hearts are opened in new ways to those for whom this is a way of life by necessity. Moreover, our planning cannot be done in isolation from the needs of our world. However little we have, even a small measure of flour and oil, we are called to share with those in need. One of the benefits of the common life lived in its fullness is that it gives us more to share.

Living the common life is rooted in compassion for the people of the future. Our freedom for mission in the future depends on our planning now, on our willingness to give everything over to the common treasury, to be responsible in our use of resources both for the sake of the community and the sake of society. It is also this compassion for those who will live in the future which leads us to "stretch our tents" and to begin to look at that broader vision of the common life which arises from collaboration with others.

Living this kind of common life is high risk living. We lose control.

We do not feather our own nest. We throw in our lot with the prophet. We let go in Gospel trust and Gospel freedom as did Dominic and Catherine, as did the widow Jesus saw in the Temple. Jesus praised the widow who "gave everything she had to live on," and Jesus's praise is blessing. Standing with that widow in her poverty and her free letting go, standing in her shoes, in her now, we too do not know the end of the story. We only know the blessing.

"McGlynn's sculpture of Dominic on the campus of Providence College portrays an intense Dominic rushing to the preaching... " This drawing of "Dominic barefoot" by Albert Carpentier, OP, also portrays a man "in a hurry" who therefore "cannot afford to be burdened with excessive baggage." (p. 127.)

20, Religious Life and the Gospel[1]

Dear Brothers,

As we approach Holy Week, the Paschal Triduum, and the Easter Season, I would like to share in this last letter to you some thoughts about religious life.

"I do it all for the sake of the gospel, that I may share in its blessings." (1 Cor 9:23).

FOR THE SAKE OF THE GOSPEL

When people hear the word "gospel," ordinarily they think of the four Gospels — a literary genre of which we have four examples in our Christian Scriptures. These four works of literature, however, have come to be called Gospels because they contain "the gospel of Jesus Christ," that is, the good news of the life, death, and resurrection of Jesus, the Christ. This is another level at which the word "gospel" can be understood. The gospel of Jesus Christ undergirds the Gospels according to Matthew, Mark, Luke, and John.

At still another level, however, we can distinguish between the gospel of Jesus Christ understood as the gospel *about* Jesus Christ (Jesus Christ being the object of preaching) and the gospel of Jesus Christ understood as the good news that Jesus himself preached. This latter is the "gospel of God" that Jesus preached before he died and was raised from the dead. This is the gospel that Jesus made incarnate in his own life. In this use, Jesus is the subject, the Preacher. The object of the preaching is God: Jesus' experience, image, and understanding of God.

"The gospel of God" is a New Testament expression. Paul refers to it (Rom 1:1, 15:1), and in the Gospel of Mark, we have Jesus returning to Galilee after the death of John the Baptist where Jesus preaches the gospel of God (Mk 1:14).

There are three levels then at which we can understand the word "gospel": a particular literary form (the four Gospels), the story of Jesus as the Christ of God (the gospel about Jesus), and the God whom Jesus proclaimed and to whom he gave witness (the gospel of God). Ultimately, the gospel *is* God — God experienced and proclaimed as good news.

Since the gospel plays such a significant role in our lives, it is worthwhile for us to take time to state succinctly what the gospel of God

1. March 19, 1994, Feast of St. Joseph

is for which Jesus gave his life and to which we have given ours. In one sentence, what, in your experience and understanding, is the gospel?

If we were to ask Paul, he would say something about the power of God, that the gospel of God is the power of God, that God is strong. According to Mark, the gospel of God is the nearness of God: the good news that God is close at hand. For Luke, God is compassionate and merciful. The good news for Matthew is that God is both just and generous (grace): the new Torah. For John, God is love. Whether we talk about the strength or nearness or compassion or grace or love of God, the gospel is about God. The gospel is God, God as close, as merciful, etc. Who is the God whom we preach and to whom we bear witness?

Although we talk about our lives in varying ways, for me it has become most meaningful to speak about living for the sake of the gospel. This Pauline expression is rich with symbolic power. It says it all.

At times people speak about celibacy for the sake of the kingdom (Matt 19:10-12). Although the expression "kingdom of God" is prevalent in the New Testament and in the preaching of Jesus, I prefer the expression "for the sake of the gospel." It is easier to articulate its meaning in our contemporary world. In the end, "the kingdom of God" is "the gospel of God" and both refer to God. The kingdom *is* God. Jesus preached God. God was the content of Jesus' preaching, the motive for Jesus' preaching, the source of Jesus' preaching. To live for the sake of the gospel is to live for God. As it was later said of Dominic, it could have been said of Jesus: he talked only to God and about God. Likewise for us: we live for the gospel.

THE GOSPEL AND THE CHURCH

One cannot live for the gospel without also living as Church. Evangelical people are also ecclesial people, and vice versa. "Church" is a complex reality, and I will only make two points here.

1. *The Gospel Necessitates or Requires Church.* I am not identifying the word "church" at this point with any particular church or ecclesial tradition, nor with any particular way of being structured. "Church" refers to communities of faith or communities of the faithful. It implies both people and structures — people of faith, the structures of community. However the church may be structured, in whatever culture or whatever period of history, there is the underlying reality of the solidarity of the faithful for mission. The gospel cannot be lived as isolated, atomistic units. The gospel creates a people — an evangelical people, an ecclesial people.

In contemporary times it has become commonplace among some to oppose the gospel and the church. Many say, gospel yes, church no. Others feel that the church comes first, then the gospel. However this tension manifests itself in the concrete, the two cannot be ultimately opposed because there is no gospel without church, or church without gospel. Each requires the other.

Historically, however one reconstructs Christian origins, the Jesus movement became church. Communities of faith resulted from the proclamation of the gospel and the celebration of the Lord's Supper. These communities became the bearers and witnesses of the tradition. The gospel today is available to us only because of this tradition. The proclamation gave birth to communities and these communities preserved and handed on the proclamation. The gospel gave birth to the church (ecclesial communities) and continued to live because of the church.

The "gospel" requires "church," however that church might structure itself. It is not particular historical structures that the church requires but simply the fact of being structured. Without structures, there is no community. Any movement eventually requires structure, rituals, institutional forms if the cause is to go on. People don't exist in a social vacuum.

This says nothing about how church might be structured, or ought to be structured, or ought not be structured, or the need or lack of need for reform of church structures. There have in fact been varied ecclesial traditions, and in the Catholic tradition the church has been variously structured at different periods of history. Structurally the church of the thirteenth century was not the church of the second century nor the church of the nineteenth century.

The point I am making is that the gospel requires structures for its own sake. I can't say "gospel yes, church no." One doesn't live the gospel completely unchurched. To give oneself to the gospel is to give oneself to church — to building up communities of faith — basic ecclesial communities. The Word becomes enfleshed in the life of a community.

2. *The Church is Always Inadequate to the Gospel.* Although the church or a community is where the gospel is alive, nevertheless the church or ecclesial communities can never do justice to the fullness of the gospel. There is always "more" to the gospel (a surplus if you will) than the church can do justice to. In that sense, people of the gospel will always be disappointed with church at the same time that they need and see the need for church.

In many ways this is obvious. Yet it can be difficult to acknowledge. Or perhaps we never realized it before. How we cope with our disappointment is another topic. That such disappointment should exist, however, is not surprising.

There is simply more to the gospel than any human society or community can attain. We only approximate, or attain intermittently or inconsistently, what the gospel calls for, calls forth. Since the gospel *is*, in one real sense, God, we never do full justice to God. There is always something or someone calling us forward into ever stronger solidarity with God and solidarity with others.

This is true no matter how the church gets structured. Any structural change one might imagine will inevitably fall short of gospel fullness. If, for example, a century from now the church were to be structured significantly differently along more egalitarian lines, it will still be inadequate to the gospel.

This realization should not make us indifferent to reforming church structures. Reform at times may be a moral imperative. There is no excuse for apathy. Whatever the consequences of our human re-structuring, however, the church will still not be all that the gospel is. Until the Parousia, there will always be a surplus in the gospel. There will be needs unmet, people on a periphery, values not fully embodied, differences of perspective and emphasis, the cry for a justice only God can give, sin at odds with grace. There will always be more — there is a surplus — that will stand as a critique, as a challenge, as a call to the church.

There is a reciprocal but unequal relationship between gospel and church. We live for the gospel; we live as church. As church, we are constantly aware of our inadequacy and of the surplus inherent in the gospel: the "more" that calls us forth.

RELIGIOUS LIFE: ATTENTIVENESS TO THE SURPLUS IN THE GOSPEL

The identity of religious, their role in the life of the church, and the charisms which the varied forms of religious life embody are much discussed today. I myself see the specificity of religious life coming from its attentiveness to the surplus in the gospel. The primary concern and focus for religious life is the gospel. We live for the sake of the gospel, and specifically the surplus in the gospel.

No matter how the church is structured, it calls people forth to be of service — within the context of ecclesial structures. But there will remain still more to the gospel. Hence the gospel requires other structures or movements that attend to this "remainder" or this "surplus." Religious life is simply the history of such movements. This is why there will always be religious life — whatever shapes or forms it takes. The Holy Spirit raises up movements of people within the church whose specific purpose is attentiveness to the surplus in the gospel. This has four implications.

1. *Religious life is essential to the church.* Religious life is not simply a nice addition or an alternative life style. The Holy Spirit calls forth religious life — historically, primarily lay movements — for the sake of the gospel. The gospel requires not only church and thus the core structures of the church but also interrelated structures and movements so that the gospel in its fullness might be better served. These structures are essential for the ecclesial expression of the full gospel.

2. *Religious life, while essential to the church, is not structurally central in the church, but rather peripheral to the basic structures of the church.* This is not to contradict myself. This insight is important for understanding religious life. "Peripheral" does *not* mean unimportant, inessential, or superfluous. Religious life is essential. It is significant. It is not, however, at the center of the basic structures of the church — no matter how the church has been or will be structured. The desire of a religious is never to be at the heart of the church structures. This is why Dominic did not want to be a bishop. Being a bishop is a valid but different calling and is only acceptable for a religious as a rare exception. It is essential to religious life to be at the periphery of the structures of the church. We ought never envy those who are at the center of those structures. Such is not our charism. We are peripheral to the core structures of the church — at the heart of the gospel but not at the heart of church structure.

3. *We are who we are and where we are because our primary allegiance or loyalty is to the gospel* — not to the structures of the church or even the church — although gospel and church can never be dichotomized. A bishop's primary loyalty, a priest's primary loyalty, within the present structures of the church, is to the church — to the gospel to be sure, but the gospel as viewed from within the structure of the church. A bishop is a churchman — in the best sense of that term. But a religious is an evangelist — in the fullest sense of that term. Religious life is part of the charismatic history of the church. The raison d'être for religious life is the primacy it gives to the gospel. We live for the sake of the gospel. All baptized Christians do this. We, however, do it with a particular intentionality.

4. *That which specifically defines us is not simply gospel as such but the surplus in the gospel.* Part of our crisis of identity is an inability to see clearly what we are specifically about within the church. Many may feel, if there were no religious, or if some day there are no religious, so what? Will the church or world be any worse off? Yes, because the gospel will be worse off, less well served. We are called by the Holy Spirit specifically to keep our focus on the gospel and the surplus in the gospel. This is our function, our purpose, our responsibility. If we don't do it, who will? The surplus in the gospel will be neglected and the gospel itself suffer damage. We are called specifically to keep our gaze on the gospel and to define ourselves in terms of the gospel surplus from within the context of our own particular charism.

We could ask a further question which space does not allow us to answer here. Within religious life, what specifically is the charism of the Preacher? All religious are defined by their relationship to the gospel and the surplus in the gospel. What specifically within the surplus in the gospel gives Dominican life and mission its identity and focus?

Perhaps these reflections can stimulate further conversations. What do we say that the gospel is? What is the *raison d' être* for religious life? What is our responsibility within the church? To what, or rather to whom, do our lives give witness?

1. March 19, 1994, Feast of St. Joseph
In the risen Christ,
Your brother,
Don